THE ULTIMATE BIRD WATCHING BOOK FOR KIDS

EXPLORE, LEARN, AND JOURNAL 50 AMAZING BACKYARD BIRDS FOR KIDS

COLORED INTERIOR

DR. FANATOMY

copyright@ dr. fanatomy 2024

All rights reserved. No part of this publication may be reproduced, distributed, or transmitted in any form or by any means, including photocopying, recording, or other electronic or mechanical methods, without the prior written permission of the publisher, except in the case of brief quotations embodied in critical reviews and certain other noncommercial uses permitted by copyright law.

This book is a work of non-fiction , and any resemblance to actual persons, living or dead, or actual events is purely coincidental.

The information and techniques described in this book are intended for educational and informational purposes only. The author and publisher shall not be held liable for any injury, damage, or loss arising from the use or misuse of the information presented in this book.

While every effort has been made to ensure the accuracy of the information contained within this book, the author and publisher make no warranties or representations, express or implied, about the completeness, accuracy, reliability, suitability, or availability with respect to the contents of this book for any purpose. The use of any information provided in this book is at the reader's own risk.

TABLE OF CONTENTS

1. WELCOME TO THE WONDERFUL WORLD OF BIRDS!
(Pg 4-8)

- WHAT IS BIRDWATCHING?
- WHY ARE BIRDS SO COOL?
- BIRDWATCHING: UNLOCK YOUR INNER NATURE NINJA
- FUN CORNER 1

2. BECOMING A BACKYARD BIRD DETECTIVE (Pg 9-16)

- MAKING A BIRDWATCHING KIT FOR KIDS!
- DRESSING FOR THE BIRDING ADVENTURE
- BIRDING ETIQUETTE: THE CODE OF THE BACKYARD BIRD DETECTIVE
- FUN CORNER 2

3. BIRDING BASICS FOR YOUNG ORNITHOLOGISTS
(Pg 17-26)

- COOL BIRD BODY PARTS
- HANDY BIRD WORDS
- BIRD IDENTIFICATION TIPS: SIZE, SHAPE, COLOR, AND BEHAVIOR
- FUN CORNER 3

4. BACKYARD BIRD BONANZA:
(AN ILLUSTRATED GUIDE TO 50 COMMON BACKYARD BIRDS)

GROUP 1: COLORFUL BIRDS
(Pg 27-87)

- NORTHERN CARDINAL (CARDINALIS CARDINALIS)
- AMERICAN GOLDFINCH (SPINUS TRISTIS)
- BALTIMORE ORIOLE (ICTERUS GALBULA)
- BLUE JAY (CYANOCITTA CRISTATA)
- EASTERN BLUEBIRD (SIALIA SIALIS)

TABLE OF CONTENTS

GROUP 2: SMALL BIRDS

- HOUSE FINCH (HAEMORHOUS MEXICANUS)
- BLACK-CAPPED CHICKADEE (POECILE ATRICAPILLUS)
- AMERICAN ROBIN (TURDUS MIGRATORIUS)
- DARK-EYED JUNCO (JUNCO HYEMALIS)
- SONG SPARROW (MELOSPIZA MELODIA)

GROUP 3: WOODPECKERS

- DOWNY WOODPECKER (DRYOBATES PUBESCENS)
- HAIRY WOODPECKER (LEUCONOTOPICUS VILLOSUS)
- NORTHERN FLICKER (COLAPTES AURATUS)
- RED-BELLIED WOODPECKER (MELANERPES CAROLINUS)
- PILEATED WOODPECKER (DRYOCOPUS PILEATUS)

GROUP 4: WATER BIRDS

- MALLARD DUCK (ANAS PLATYRHYNCHOS)
- GREAT BLUE HERON (ARDEA HERODIAS)
- CANADA GOOSE (BRANTA CANADENSIS)
- AMERICAN COOT (FULICA AMERICANA)
- WOOD DUCK (AIX SPONSA)

GROUP 5: BIRDS OF PREY

- RED-TAILED HAWK (BUTEO JAMAICENSIS)
- AMERICAN KESTREL (FALCO SPARVERIUS)
- GREAT HORNED OWL (BUBO VIRGINIANUS)
- BARN OWL (TYTO ALBA)
- BALD EAGLE (HALIAEETUS LEUCOCEPHALUS)

GROUP 6: GROUND FEEDERS

- NORTHERN BOBWHITE (COLINUS VIRGINIANUS)
- EASTERN TOWHEE (PIPILO ERYTHROPHTHALMUS)
- WILD TURKEY (MELEAGRIS GALLOPAVO)
- KILLDEER (CHARADRIUS VOCIFERUS)
- MOURNING DOVE (ZENAIDA MACROURA)

TABLE OF CONTENTS

GROUP 7: SINGING BIRDS

- NORTHERN MOCKINGBIRD (MIMUS POLYGLOTTOS)
- HOUSE WREN (TROGLODYTES AEDON)
- GRAY CATBIRD (DUMETELLA CAROLINENSIS)
- EASTERN MEADOWLARK (STURNELLA MAGNA)
- WOOD THRUSH (HYLOCICHLA MUSTELINA)

GROUP 8: SEASONAL VISITORS

- RUBY-THROATED HUMMINGBIRD (ARCHILOCHUS COLUBRIS)
- CEDAR WAXWING (BOMBYCILLA CEDRORUM)
- SNOWY OWL (BUBO SCANDIACUS)
- AMERICAN TREE SPARROW (SPIZELLOIDES ARBOREA)
- YELLOW-RUMPED WARBLER (SETOPHAGA CORONATA)

GROUP 9: SOCIAL BIRDS

- EUROPEAN STARLING (STURNUS VULGARI)
- HOUSE SPARROW (PASSER DOMESTICUS)
- COMMON GRACKLE (QUISCALUS QUISCULA)
- AMERICAN CROW (CORVUS BRACHYRHYNCHOS)
- RED-WINGED BLACKBIRD (AGELAIUS PHOENICEUS)

GROUP 10: BIRDS WITH UNIQUE FEATURES

- BELTED KINGFISHER (MEGACERYLE ALCYON)
- RED-HEADED WOODPECKER (MELANERPES ERYTHROCEPHALUS)
- EASTERN PHOEBE (SAYORNIS PHOEBE)
- WHITE-BREASTED NUTHATCH (SITTA CAROLINENSIS)
- CAROLINA WREN (THRYOTHORUS LUDOVICIANUS)

Fun Corner 4

5. THE AMAZING WORLD OF BIRDS (Pg 88-94)

- SUPERPOWERS OF BIRDS
- BIRDS AND THE ENVIRONMENT
- THREATS BIRDS FACE
- HABITAT LOSS
- FUN CORNER 5

TABLE OF CONTENTS

6. BECOME A BIRDING MASTER! (Pg 95-101)

- KEEPING A BIRDING JOURNAL
- BIRD PHOTOGRAPHY BASICS
- BUILD A PINECONE BIRD FEEDER
- CREATE A BIRD BATH
- PLANT BIRD-FRIENDLY PLANTS
- FUN CORNER 6

7. APPENDIX AND CONCLUSION (Pg 102-107)

- GLOSSARY 1: BIRDING TERMS
- GLOSSARY 2: ONLINE RESOURCES & BIRDING APPS FOR KIDS
- CONCLUSION: YOUR BIRDWATCHING ADVENTURE AWAITS!

Get ready to dive into the fantastic world of birds! In this chapter, you'll learn what birdwatching is, why birds are super cool, and how easy and fun it is to start birdwatching. Let's explore the wonders of our feathered friends and start your birdwatching adventure!

What is Birdwatching?

Birdwatching, or birding, is a fun and exciting hobby where you observe and study birds in their natural habitats. Here's what makes birdwatching awesome:

- <u>Anywhere, Anytime</u>: You can birdwatch in your backyard, neighborhood park, or even faraway forests and wetlands.
- <u>Observe and Learn</u>: Respond to birds' colors, shapes, sizes, movements, and calls.
- Discover Behaviors: Learn about what birds eat, how they build nests and their unique behaviors.
- <u>Keep a Record</u>: Take notes, draw pictures, or keep a "life list" of all the birds you see.
- <u>Like a Treasure Hunt</u>: Each bird you find is a new and exciting discovery!

Pharaoh Power! Ancient Egyptians weren't just watching birds, they kept falcons as hunting pets!

Why Are Birds So Cool?

<u>Incredible Diversity</u>: Birds are like living rainbows in the animal kingdom. From the minuscule hummingbird that weighs less than a nickel to the enormous ostrich that towers over us, the size difference is mind-boggling!

The hummingbird's tiny heart beats up to 1,200 times per minute - faster than a race car engine!

Why Are Birds So Cool?..continued

<u>Unique Abilities</u>: Birds are nature's superheroes! Take the Arctic Tern, for example. This champion migrator flies 22,000 miles yearly, journeying from the Arctic to Antarctica and back again. Their unique facial features act like satellite dishes, pinpointing even the faintest squeak of a mouse in the dead of night. Talk about super hearing!

<u>Beautiful Songs:</u> Birds are the original rockstars of the animal kingdom. Each species has its unique song, a kind of feathered symphony. Did you know that some bird songs are so complex that they sound like music composed by a human? The mockingbird, for instance, can mimic the sounds of other birds, cars honking, and even human speech!

<u>Birds are like nature's helpers</u>: They visit flowers, drink nectar, and pick up pollen on their feathers. When they see another flower, they spread pollen, helping plants make seeds. Birds also eat bugs that can harm our gardens and crops, keeping them safe and healthy.

Birds are not just amazing in real life; they also inspire our art, stories, and myths. For example, in ancient Greece, owls were seen as wise, so they were often with the goddess of knowledge. In many cultures, doves mean peace, and eagles stand for strength. Birds keep inspiring artists and writers everywhere. So, get ready to learn lots of cool stuff as you start birdwatching!

Long ago, in ancient Greece, people thought owls were the smartest birds around. They even thought they were the symbol of wisdom!

Arctic Tern
Pic Credit- Pixabay

Birdwatching: Unlock Your Inner Nature Ninja!

Calling all future explorers and nature enthusiasts! Birdwatching is a secret weapon disguised as a super fun hobby. Here's why it's the perfect training ground for young nature ninjas like you:

- Sharpen Your Observation Skills: Birdwatching is like detective work for the outdoors! You'll use your keen eyes and quiet movements to spot birds camouflaged in trees or flitting through bushes. The more you practice, the better you'll notice tiny details, like the f of a blue jay's wing or the delicate curve of a hummingbird's bec

- Patience is a Superpower: Birds aren't always in a hurry to put show. Sometimes, you might need to wait quietly for a feath friend to appear. But that's okay! Learning patience is a valu skill, and birdwatching teaches you to appreciate the calmness beauty of nature, even when things are quiet.

- Become a Bird Language Expert: Did you know birds have their secret language? Birdwatching helps you decode their chirps, whistles, and songs. Imagine learning to identify different bird species just by the sounds they make! It's like becoming a bird translator, understanding their conversations and calls.

- Knowledge is Power: The more birds you see, the more you learn about their fantastic world. You'll discover different bird habitats, what they eat, and how they raise their young. Birdwatching turns you into a walking encyclopedia of feathered facts, ready to impress your friends and family with your knowledge!

- Team Up and Share the Adventure: Birdwatching can be a solo quest, but it's even more fun with friends! Join a local birdwatching club or connect with online communities. Sharing your discoveries with others and learning from experienced birdwatchers will make your adventures even more exciting.

Fun Corner 1

Did You Know

- <u>Pigeon Racing</u>: Did you know that pigeons can race? Some pigeons have been known to fly up to 600 miles to get back home, and there are even pigeon racing competitions!

- <u>Bird with Boots</u> The Secretarybird, found in Africa, has long legs that look like it's wearing boots. It uses these legs to stomp on its prey!

- <u>Woodpecker's Tongue</u>: A woodpecker's tongue can be up to three times the length of its beak. It wraps around its skull when not in use – talk about tongue-tied!

- <u>Dancing Birds</u>: Some birds, like the Manakin, perform elaborate dance routines to impress their mates. They can moonwalk better than Michael Jackson!

- <u>Owl's Eye Conundrum</u>: Owls can't move their eyes. Instead, they have to turn their entire head to look around – and they can turn it almost all the way around!

- <u>Birds and Dinosaurs</u>: Chickens are the closest living relatives to the Tyrannosaurus Rex. So, next time you see a chicken, imagine a tiny T-Rex!

Photo by Ansie Potgieter on Unsplash

Photo by Patrice Bouchard on Unsplash

Congratulations, junior birder! You've unlocked the exciting world of birdwatching. It's time to transform your backyard into a birding paradise and embark on thrilling feathered friend adventures. But before you head out, let's gather your essential tools and become stealthy backyard bird detectives!

Making a Birdwatching Kit for Kids!

(1) Binoculars: Your Super Secret Weapon

Binoculars help you get a clearer view of distant birds in the sky.
- <u>What They Are</u>: Binoculars help you see birds up close, even if they're far away.
- <u>How to Use</u>: Hold them to your eyes and adjust the focus until you see clearly.
- <u>Interesting Fact</u>: Did you know that some birds, like eagles, have four to five times sharper vision than humans?

(2) Field Guide: Your Birding Bible

- <u>What It Is</u>: A book with pictures and information about different birds.
- <u>How to Use</u>: Look up the birds you see to learn their names and cool facts about them.
- <u>Interesting Fact</u>: There are over 10,000 bird species in the world! Your field guide helps you identify the ones in your area.

(3) Notebook: Your Detective's Notebook

- <u>What It Is</u>: A place to record your bird sightings and observations.
- <u>How to Use</u>: Could you write down the date, time, location, and what the bird was doing? You can even draw pictures!
- <u>Interesting Fact</u>: Keeping a bird journal can help scientists learn more about bird habits. You might contribute to the necessary research!

(4) Bird Feeder: Feathered Friends Welcome!

- <u>What It Is</u>: A feeder that holds bird food and attracts birds to your backyard.
- <u>How to Use</u>: Fill it with birdseed and hang it in a tree or on a hook outside.
- <u>Interesting Fact</u>: Different birds like different types of seeds. Experiment to see who visits your feeder!

Platform Feeder Tube Feeder Suet Feeder Hopper Feeder

(5) Smartphone App: Techie Birdwatching

- <u>What It Is</u>: An app that helps you identify birds by their calls or songs.
- <u>How to Use</u>: Open the app and listen to the bird sounds. Match what you hear to the app's recordings.
- <u>Interesting Fact</u>: Some birds have songs with hundreds of different notes!

App	How It Works	Bird Types Covered	Cool Features	Easy to Use?	Community Fun
Merlin Bird ID	Works offline & online	Many birds	Identifies birds by photo and sound	Yes	Yes, lots of users
Audubon Bird Guide	Mostly offline	Many birds	Identifies birds by photo and sound	Yes	Not much
eBird by Cornell	Mostly online	Birds all over the world	Shows bird sightings on maps	Yes	Yes, lots of users
iBird Pro Guide	Mostly offline	Many birds	Photos, sounds, detailed info	Yes	Not much
BirdNET	Online only	Focus on bird sounds	Identifies birds by sound	Very simple	Not much

(6) Small Camera: Capture the Moment

- <u>What It Is</u>: A camera to take photos of the birds you spot.
- <u>How to Use</u>: Take pictures from a distance so you don't scare the birds away.
- <u>Interesting Fact</u>: Bird photographers sometimes spend hours waiting for the perfect shot!

(7) Backpack: Pack It All Up

- <u>What It Is</u>: A small backpack to carry all your birdwatching gear.
- <u>How to Use</u>: Pack your binoculars, field guide, notebook, water bottle, and snacks.
- <u>Interesting Fact</u>: Birdwatchers often hike to find rare birds, so a backpack is handy!

Birdwatching Kit Checklist

Item	Use	Fun Fact
Binoculars	See birds up close	Eagles have vision up to four times sharper than humans!
Field Guide	Identify and learn about birds	There are over 10,000 bird species in the world!
Notebook	Record bird sightings and notes	Your bird journal can help scientists with research!
Bird Feeder	Attract birds to your backyard	Different birds prefer different seeds. Experiment to find their favorites!
Smartphone App	Identify birds by their calls	Some birds have songs with hundreds of different notes!
Small Camera	Take photos of birds	Bird photographers sometimes spend hours waiting for the perfect shot!
Backpack	Carry all your gear	Birdwatchers often hike to find rare birds.

Dressing for the Birding Adventure:

Be a Nature Ninja

- Dress for comfort and camouflage. Opt for neutral colors like greens, browns, and beiges to blend in with the environment. This will help you avoid startling the birds you're trying to observe.

Weather or Not You'll Go Birding:

- Always check the weather forecast before heading out. Dress in layers to adjust to changing temperatures. Remember a hat, sunscreen, and insect repellent (if necessary).

Footwear Fit for a Nature Explorer:

- Comfortable shoes are essential! Hiking boots or sturdy sneakers will provide proper traction for uneven terrain.

- Bonus Tip: Pack a small backpack to carry your binoculars, field guide, notebook, water bottle, and any other essentials you might need on your birding adventure.

Birding Etiquette: The Code of the Backyard Bird Detective

Birdwatching is all about respecting wildlife and their habitats. Here are some essential birding etiquette tips to remember:

- <u>Be a Silent Observer</u>: Birds are easily startled by loud noises. Talk softly and move slowly to avoid disturbing them.
- <u>Leave No Trace</u>: Always pack out any trash you bring with you. Respect the environment and leave the area as you find it.
- <u>Observe from a Distance</u>: Use your binoculars to get a closer look instead of approaching birds directly. This gives them the space they need to feel safe.
- <u>Feeder Fun, the Right Way</u>: Keep your bird feeder clean and filled with fresh seeds. Don't use treated wood for feeders, as it can harm birds.
- <u>Respect Nesting Sites</u>: If you find a bird's nest, admire it from afar and avoid disturbing the parents or their young.

By following these simple rules, you can ensure a positive birding experience for yourself and the feathered residents of your backyard. Now that you're equipped with the essential gear, know-how, and birding code, you're ready to step outside and transform your backyard into a birding haven!

LOL!

What's a birdwatching kid's favorite type of math?

Owl-gebra!

Why did the birdwatching kid bring a ladder to the park?

Because he wanted to see the birds on a higher level!

Fun Corner 2

Match the Beak Type to Birds

BEAK TYPE

- Strong and Short: Ideal for cracking nuts and seeds
- Long and Curved: Perfect for reaching deep into flowers for nectar
- Sharp and Hooked: Designed for tearing flesh
- Wide and Flat with Lamellae: Acts like a sieve for filtering food from water
- Long and Pointed: Excellent for probing mud or water to find hidden food
- Powerful and Scissor-like: Strong for cracking nuts, seeds, and tough fruits
- Wading and Straining: Bent for filtering tiny organisms from water
- Brush-tipped and Pollen-collecting: Helps collect pollen while sipping nectar
- Sharp and Pointed for Fishing: Designed for spearing fish
- Hooked for Scavenging: Perfect for tearing flesh from dead animals

Macaw

Flamingo

Eagle

Sparrow

Birds (Options)

Hummingbird

Sandpiper

Vulture

Duck

Kingfisher

Solution: Match the Beak Type to Birds
BEAK TYPE

- Strong and Short: Ideal for cracking nuts and seeds - sparrow

- Long and Curved: Perfect for reaching deep into flowers for nectar - hummingbird

- Sharp and Hooked: Designed for tearing flesh - eagle

- Wide and Flat with Lamellae: Acts like a sieve for filtering food from water - duck

- Long and Pointed: Excellent for probing mud or water to find hidden food - sandpiper

- Powerful and Scissor-like: Strong for cracking nuts, seeds, and tough fruits - macaw

- Wading and Straining: Bent for filtering tiny organisms from water - flamingo

- Brush-tipped and Pollen-collecting: Helps collect pollen while sipping nectar - hummingbirds

- Sharp and Pointed for Fishing: Designed for spearing fish - kingfishers

- Hooked for Scavenging: Perfect for tearing flesh from dead animals - vultures

Welcome to the world of birding! In this chapter, you'll discover the essential skills every young ornithologist needs to start their bird-watching adventure. From choosing the right gear to understanding bird behavior, get ready to dive into our feathered friends' exciting and colorful realm.

Cool Bird Body Parts

(1) The Bill (or Beak)

Sparrow

Hummingbird

What It Is: The bill is a bird's mouth, used for eating, grooming, and manipulating objects.

What it does: Different shapes help birds with specific diets and activities.
- Seed-eaters: Birds like sparrows have thick bills to crack seeds.
- Insect-eaters: Birds like hummingbirds have long, pointed bills to catch bugs.

Fun Fact: A woodpecker's bill is super strong, allowing it to peck wood without hurting itself!

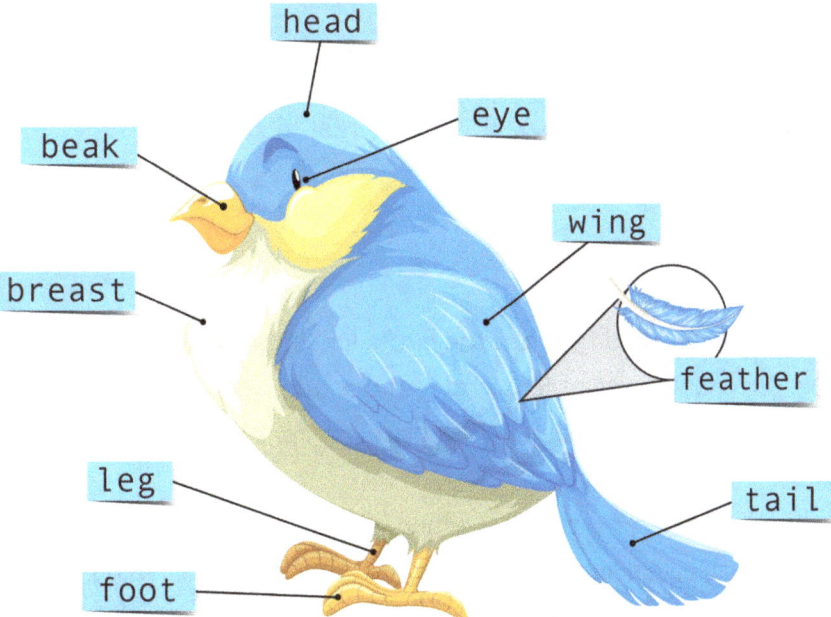
Parts of an Bird

18

(2) Wings

<u>What They Are</u>: Wings are the limbs birds use to fly.

<u>Function</u>: Wing shapes help birds with their specific flying needs.

- Songbirds: Like robins, have short, rounded wings to dart through trees.
- Hawks: Have broad wings to soar high in the sky.

<u>Fun Fact</u>: Some birds can fly up to 60 miles per hour!

(3) Tail

Swallow with black forked tail

Owl with short tail

- <u>What It Is</u>: The tail is the set of feathers at the end of a bird's body.
- <u>Function</u>: Helps with balance and steering during flight.
- <u>Long Tails</u>: Swallows have long, forked tails for fast, agile flying.
- <u>Short Tails</u>: Owls have short tails for silent, stealthy flight.
- <u>Fun Fact</u>: The tail feathers of a peacock can be over 5 feet long!

(4) Legs and Feet

- <u>What They Are</u>: Legs and feet are the bird's limbs for walking, perching, or swimming.
- <u>Function</u>: Different types of legs and feet are adapted for various activities.
- <u>Perching Birds</u>: Like bluebirds, they have three toes forward and one back to grip branches.
- <u>Wading Birds</u>: Like herons, they have long legs to walk through water.
- <u>Swimming Birds</u>: Like ducks, they have webbed feet for swimming.
- <u>Fun Fact</u>: The ostrich has the most enormous bird feet, perfect for running fast!

Webbed Feet for swimming Birds

Perching Birds

Running Birds : Ostrich

Wading Birds- Long Feet:

(5) Plumage (Feathers)

- <u>What It Is</u>: Plumage refers to a bird's feathers.
- <u>Function</u>: Feathers serve multiple purposes.
- <u>Insulation</u>: Keeps birds warm.
- <u>Camouflage</u>: Helps birds blend into their surroundings.
- <u>Waterproofing</u>: Keeps birds dry.
- <u>Fun Fact</u>: Male birds often have brighter plumage than females to attract mates!

Handy Bird Words

Field guides and birding apps use special terms to describe bird features. Knowing these will make you a bird ID pro!

Term	Location	Fun Fact
Crown	Top of the head	Birds can raise their crown feathers to show excitement!
Nape	Back of the neck	The nape feathers can be a different color, like a hidden spot!
Lores	Between the bill and the eye	Some birds have colorful lores, like a masked superhero!
Rump	Between the back and the tail	Often hidden, but can be a bright flash of color in flight!
Flanks	Sides of the body below the wings	Flanks help with balance during tricky maneuvers!
Breast	Underside between the neck and belly	Look here for special patterns or colors!
Barring	Horizontal stripes on feathers	These stripes can make a bird look bigger to predators!
Streaking	Vertical stripes on feathers	Streaks can help with camouflage in grass and trees!
Patch	Solid area of color on the plumage	Patches can be like a bird's signature marking!

Bird Identification Tips: Size, Shape, Color, and Behavior

Identifying birds can feel like being a detective! Here are some tips to help you recognize different birds by looking at their size, shape, color, and behavior.

Size

Bee Hummingbird

What to Look For: Compare the bird to something familiar.
- <u>Example</u>: Is the bird the size of a sparrow, robin, or crow?
- <u>Fun Fact</u>: The smallest bird in the world is the bee hummingbird, about the size of a large bumblebee!
- <u>Trivia</u>: The ostrich is the most giant bird, standing up to 9 feet tall!

Bird Identification Tips: Size, Shape, Color, and Behavior..continued

Size Chart:

Bird	Size
Hummingbird	2-4 inches
Sparrow	5-7 inches
Robin	8-11 inches
Crow	16-21 inches
Hawk	18-26 inches
Ostrich	Up to 9 feet

Shape

What to Look For: Notice the bird's overall shape and specific parts like the bill and tail.

- <u>Example</u>: Does the bird have a chunky body like a pigeon or a sleek body like a falcon?
- <u>Fun Fact</u>: Birds of prey like eagles have solid and hooked bills for tearing meat.
- <u>Trivia</u>: The albatross has the longest wingspan of any bird, reaching up to 11 feet!

Shape Features:

Feature	Bird Example	Description
Bill	Pelican	Long, pouch-like bill
Wings	Swift	Long, narrow wings for fast flying
Tail	Woodpecker	Stiff tail feathers for support on trees
Body	Duck	Streamlined body for swimming

Color

- <u>What to Look For</u>: Check the colors and patterns on the bird's feathers.
- <u>Example</u>: Is the bird all one color or has spots, stripes, or patches?
- <u>Fun Fact</u>: Male cardinals are bright red, while females are brown with hints of red.
- <u>Trivia</u>: The peacock's dazzling tail feathers are used to attract mates!

Color Patterns:

Pattern	Bird Example	Description
Solid	Blue Jay	Entirely blue with white patches
Spotted	Starling	Black with white spots
Striped	Zebra Finch	Horizontal stripes on the chest
Patches	American Robin	Red breast, brown back

Behavior

- What to Look For: Observe what the bird is doing—how it flies, feeds, and interacts with others.
- Example: Does the bird hop on the ground, perch on branches, or soar high in the sky?
- Fun Fact: Some birds, like the Arctic Tern, migrate thousands of miles yearly!
- Trivia: Crows are known for their intelligence and can even use tools to find food.

Behavior Traits:

Behavior	Bird Example	Description
Feeding	Woodpecker	Drills into trees to find insects
Flying	Hummingbird	Hovers in mid-air while feeding on nectar
Socializing	Parrot	Often seen in flocks, very social
Nesting	Swallow	Builds nests from mud on structures

What do you call a smart bird?

A wise quacker!

Why do seagulls fly over the sea?

Because if they flew over the bay, they'd be bagels!

Quiz Corner

1. What feature helps birds keep warm?
   a) Beak b) Wings c) Plumage d) Tail

2. Which bird is known for having the longest tail feathers?
   a) Hummingbird b) Sparrow c) Peacock d) Robin

3. What type of feet do ducks have?
   a) Clawed feet b) Webbed feet c) Perching feet d) Running feet

4. What is the purpose of a bird's tail during flight?
   a) Singing b) Steering and balance c) Eating d) Sleeping

5. Which bird is the smallest in the world?
   a) Robin b) Eagle c) Hummingbird d) Owl

6. What do hawks use their broad wings for?
   a) Perching b) Soaring high in the sky c) Hopping on the ground d) Building nests

7. What kind of bill do seed-eating birds have?
   a) Thick bill b) Long, pointed bill c) Flat bill d) Curved bill

8. Why do some birds have bright plumage?
   a) To stay warm b) To attract mates c) To fly faster d) To sing louder

9. What do perching birds use their feet for?
   a) Swimming b) Running c) Grasping branches d) Digging

10. Which bird is known for its intelligence and ability to use tools?
    a) Penguin b) Sparrow c) Crow (Known for problem-solving skills) d) Flamingo

Fun Corner 3

Solution: Quiz Corner

1. What feature helps birds keep warm?
a) Beak b) Wings c) Plumage (Feathers provide insulation) d) Tail

2. Which bird is known for having the longest tail feathers?
a) Hummingbird b) Sparrow c) Peacock (Males have elaborate tail displays) d) Robin

3. What type of feet do ducks have?
a) Clawed feet b) Webbed feet (For paddling in water) c) Perching feet d) Running feet

4. What is the purpose of a bird's tail during flight?
a) Singing b) Steering and balance (Helps birds maneuver in the air) c) Eating d) Sleeping

5. Which bird is the smallest in the world?
a) Robin b) Eagle c) Hummingbird (Tiny size allows for hovering) d) Owl

6. What do hawks use their broad wings for?
a) Perching b) Soaring high in the sky (Efficient for gliding long distances) c) Hopping on the ground d) Building nests

7. What kind of bill do seed-eating birds have?
a) Thick bill (Strong for cracking seeds) b) Long, pointed bill c) Flat bill d) Curved bill

8. Why do some birds have bright plumage?
a) To stay warm b) To attract mates (Colorful feathers for display) c) To fly faster d) To sing louder

9. What do perching birds use their feet for?
a) Swimming b) Running c) Grasping branches (Sharp claws for holding onto trees) d) Digging

10. Which bird is known for its intelligence and ability to use tools?
a) Penguin b) Sparrow c) Crow (Known for problem-solving skills) d) Flamingo

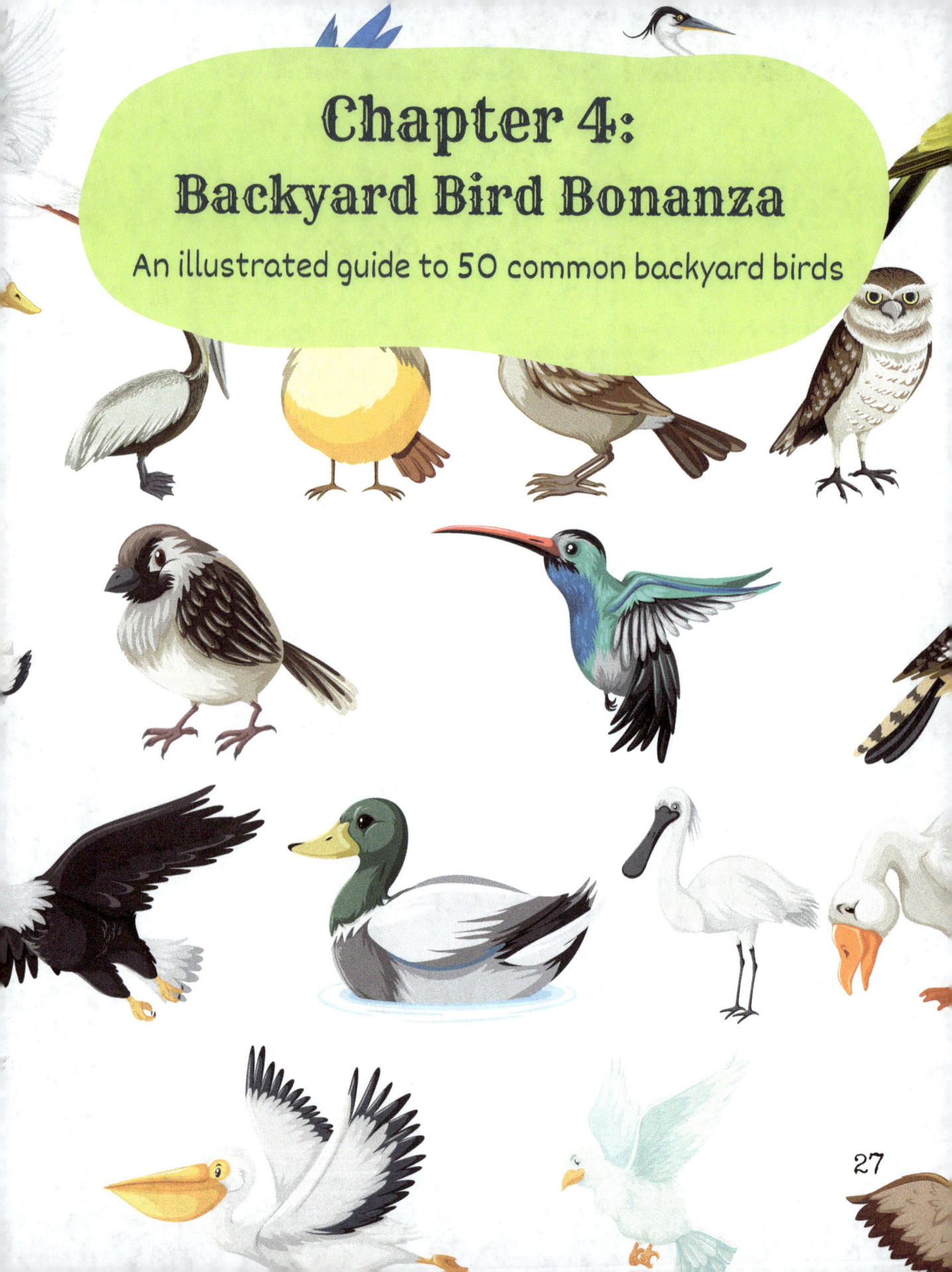

Backyard Bird Bonanza! In this exciting chapter, you'll embark on a journey to discover 50 common backyard birds. You'll learn about their size, appearance, habitats, and unique behaviors with colorful illustrations and fun facts. Get ready to become a birdwatching expert and have fun recording your sightings and observations!

Group 1: Colorful Birds

(1) Northern Cardinal (Cardinalis cardinalis)

Size and Appearance:

- Description: Males are bright red with a black mask and a spiky crest on their heads. Females are red-brown with olive accents and also have a crest.

Habitat Preferences:

- Range: Found in eastern North America, from southern Canada to Mexico.
- Preferred Habitats: woodlands, gardens, and shrublands with many bushes and trees.

Diet:

- Diet: Eat seeds, fruits, insects, grains, and nuts. They especially like sunflower and safflower seeds.

Interesting Behaviors:

- Behaviors: Known for their beautiful songs. Males sing to mark territory and attract mates. Both parents feed their young. They stay in the same area year-round, sometimes attacking their reflections in windows.

Fun Facts:

- State bird of seven U.S. states.
- Both males and females sing.
- Named for their red color, like the robes of Roman Catholic cardinals.
- Strong beaks help them crack open seeds.

Backyard Tips:

- Provide Shelter: Plant trees and bushes where they can nest. In winter, they like evergreen trees.
- Offer a Feeder: Use feeders with prominent perches and fill them with sunflower, safflower, and white milo seeds.
- Plant Berries: Grow berry bushes like dogwood.
- Avoid Reflections: Cover or remove mirrors and windows near feeding areas to stop them from attacking their reflections.

RECORD YOUR SIGHTINGS!

- Date: _____
- Location: _____
- What was the cardinal doing?: _____ _____
- Any exciting notes or observations?: _____ _____

(2) American Goldfinch (Spinus tristis):

Size and Appearance:

- Description: The American Goldfinch is a small bird with bright yellow feathers and black wings. In winter, they turn a duller brownish color.

Habitat Preferences:

- Range: They live all over North America, breeding in the northern parts and spending winters in the southern US and Mexico.
- Preferred Habitats: They like open fields, gardens, and areas with many weeds and wildflowers.

Male American Goldfinch in summer plumage

By Rodney Campbell - GoldfinchUploaded by snowmanradio, CC BY 2.0, https://commons.wikimedia.org/w/index.php?curid=20388809

Diet:

- <u>Diet</u>: Goldfinches mainly eat seeds from plants like thistles, sunflowers, and grasses. They also eat small insects and plant matter like buds and bark.

Interesting Behaviors:

- <u>Behaviors:</u> American Goldfinches are known for their bouncy flight and cheerful songs. They are late nesters, usually waiting until midsummer when their favorite plants are seeding. They can hang upside down to eat.

Fun Facts:

- They molt twice a year, changing from bright yellow in summer to dull brown in winter.
- They are also called "wild canaries" because of their bright yellow color.
- Goldfinches are very acrobatic and can cling to plants while eating.

Backyard Tips:

- <u>Provide Food</u>: Offer sunflower and Nyjer seeds in your feeders.
- <u>Choose the Right Feeder</u>: Use a feeder that allows them to climb and hang while eating.
- <u>Keep It Clean</u>: Clean feeders monthly to keep the birds healthy.
- <u>Plant Native Plants</u>: Grow thistles, milkweed, sunflowers, and other plants that produce seeds they love.

Female American Goldfinch

By Darren Swim – Own work, CC BY-SA 3.0, https://commons.wikimedia.org/w/index.php?curid=7859712

RECORD YOUR SIGHTINGS!

- Date: _____
- Location: _____
- What was the cardinal doing?: _____
  _____
- Any exciting notes or observations?: _____
  _____

(3) Baltimore Oriole (Icterus galbula):

Size and Appearance:

- <u>Description</u>: Imagine a bird dressed for a superhero party! The Baltimore Oriole is a medium-sized songbird with a fiery costume. Males are the flashiest, sporting a sleek black head contrasting with their bright orange underparts and wings. Females, on the other hand, rock a more undercover look – orange-yellow bodies with grayish wings.

Baltimore Oriole

By Darren Swim – Own work, CC BY-SA 3.0, https://commons.wikimedia.org/w/index.php?curid=7859712

Habitat Preferences:

- <u>Summertime Party Spot</u>: During the warm months, Baltimore Orioles love hanging out in eastern and central North America. They prefer open spaces with tall trees, like woodlands, forest edges, and even your backyard if it's got some remarkable trees!
- <u>Winter Migration</u>: Come winter, these birds aren't afraid of a bit of adventure. They pack their bags (or feathers?) and head south for a tropical vacation in Central America, the Caribbean, and northern South America.

Diet:

- <u>Bug Busters and Fruit Fanatics</u>: Baltimore Orioles are like the ultimate picky eaters... but not really! They're omnivores, meaning they enjoy a mix of both plants and animals. They love munching on insects – consider them nature's pest control unit! But they also have a sweet tooth for juicy fruits like oranges and love sipping nectar from flowers and feeders.

Interesting Behaviors:

- Music Makers: These birds are the rockstars of the feathery world! They're famous for their beautiful songs, often described as sweet and melodic, like a tiny flute playing a happy tune.
- Nest Architects: Orioles are master builders! They weave amazing, hanging nests from plant fibers, which they suspend from sturdy tree branches. It's like a secret treehouse for their chicks!
- Leaping Lizards (Well, Birds): Orioles are super active. They hop and flit through the treetops like tiny acrobats, always looking for their next delicious snack.

Fun Facts:

- Lord Baltimore's Legacy: Did you know these birds are named after a famous historical figure? Lord Baltimore's coat of arms had colors that looked just like the Baltimore Orioles!
- Insect Ninjas: Orioles are nature's superheroes when it comes to bugs! They gobble up tons of insects, including many that can damage plants. So, having them around is like having a natural pest control service in your backyard!
- The Power of Orange: Want to attract these dazzling birds to your yard? Think orange! Orioles are drawn to this color, so orange slices and feeders with orange accents are a surefire way to make them your backyard buddies.

Backyard Tips:

- Become an Oriole Chef: Orioles love a variety of foods. Offer them a smorgasbord of their favorites! Put out orange slices, grape jelly (yes, really!), and nectar in feeders designed for orioles. These feeders often have unique spots for both fruit and nectar.
- The Perfect Perch: Not all feeders are created equal! Choose feeders explicitly designed for orioles. These feeders have openings and perches suitable for their beaks and bodies and may even have compartments for both fruit and nectar.
- Plant a Birdie Buffet: Make your yard an Oriole paradise! Plant native trees and shrubs with delicious fruits these birds can enjoy. Don't forget to add some flowering plants that produce nectar – they'll be a sweet treat for your feathered friends.
- Birdie Bath Time: Like you, Orioles need a place to cool off and take a refreshing bath. Provide a shallow bird bath or mister in your yard. It'll be a welcome sight for these thirsty birds on a hot summer day!

RECORD YOUR SIGHTINGS!

- Date: _____
- Location: _____
- What was the cardinal doing?: _____
  _____
- Any exciting notes or observations?: _____
  _____

(4) Blue Jay (Cyanocitta cristata) :

Blue Jay

Size and Appearance:

- <u>Flashy Feathers:</u> The Blue Jay rocks a bright blue crest, black necklace, and white tummy. They're the rockstars of the backyard!

Habitat Preferences:

- <u>Found Everywhere (Almost!):</u> Blue Jays are all over eastern and central North America, from Canada to Florida and Texas. They stay put year-round but might head south for a warmer winter if things get too chilly.
- <u>Treetop Town:</u> Blue Jays love hanging out in woodlands, gardens, and backyards with plenty of trees – their high-rise apartments!

Diet:

- Snack Stashers: Blue Jays are omnivores, meaning they eat various things. They love acorns, nuts, seeds, fruits, insects, and sometimes even small animals. They're also notorious for hiding their food to eat later, like tiny squirrels!

Interesting Behaviors:

- Clever Copycats: Blue Jays are super bright! They can mimic sounds like birds and even use tools to get food.
- Talkative Troublemakers: These birds love to chat loudly, and sometimes they might even try to trick other birds with sounds like a hawk!

Fun Facts:

- Blue Jays can mimic the calls of hawks to scare other birds away from food.
- They're excellent at hiding and finding food, like acorns, which they often bury.
- They play an essential role in spreading oak trees by forgetting where they buried acorns!

Backyard Buddies:
- Feeder Frenzy: Attract Blue Jays with tray or hopper feeders filled with peanuts, sunflower seeds, or suet.
- Birdbath Bonanza: Offer a birdbath for them to drink and keep their feathers clean.
- Plant a Future Feast: Planting oak trees gives them a delicious food source for years to come.

RECORD YOUR SIGHTINGS!

- Date: _____
- Location: _____
- What was the cardinal doing?: _____
- Any exciting notes or observations?: _____

(5) Eastern Bluebird (Sialia sialis)

Size and Appearance:

- <u>Description</u>: Brilliant Blue Beauty: Eastern Bluebirds are tiny splashes of blue with a rusty red chest and a white tummy. Males wear the brightest blue, while females have a cooler shade.

Habitat Preferences:

- <u>Open Country Explorer</u>: Look for them in eastern North America, from Canada to the Gulf of Mexico. They might even stay put year-round in the south!

- <u>Tree Spotters:</u> They love open spaces like woodlands, farmlands, orchards, and even your backyard if it has some trees and open ground.

Eastern Bluebird

Diet:

- Insect-Eating Extraordinaire: These little birds are insect superheroes. They gobble up beetles, caterpillars, and grasshoppers to keep gardens healthy. In winter, they might switch to a fruity feast of berries.

Interesting Behaviors:

- <u>Sing a Happy Tune</u>: Eastern Bluebirds are famous for their cheerful songs, filling the air with happy melodies. You might see them perched on wires or branches, looking for a tasty snack.

- <u>Nest Box Champions:</u> These birds like to raise their families in cozy cavities. If you put a nest box in your yard, they might become your tenants!

Fun Facts:
- Symbol of Sunshine: Eastern Bluebirds are like little symbols of happiness, spreading joy with their bright colors and cheery songs.
- Busy Parents: They're super family-oriented birds, often raising more than one batch of chicks each year!
- Garden Guardians: By munching on insects, Bluebirds help keep gardens healthy – making them your backyard's pest control crew!

Backyard Buddies:
- A Feathery Feast: Attract them with mealworms, berries, and suet in your feeders.
- The Perfect Plate: Use platform feeders or dishes, since Bluebirds prefer open spaces to eat.
- Home Sweet Nest Box: Put up bluebird nest boxes in your yard to give them a cozy place to raise their families.
- Watery Oasis: Provide a birdbath for them to drink and keep their feathers clean.

RECORD YOUR SIGHTINGS!

- Date: _____
- Location: _____
- What was the cardinal doing?: _____
  _____
- Any exciting notes or observations?: _____
  _____

What kind of bird works at a construction site?

A Crane

Which bird always wins the acting awards?

The Mockingbird!

Group 2: Small Birds

(1) House Finch (Haemorhous mexicanus)

Size and Appearance:

- Red-Headed Charmer: House Finches are small songbirds with bright red heads and chests. Males wear a bolder red, while females wear a blend of brown and streaky markings.

House Finch

Habitat Preferences:

- City Slicker Songbird: Look for them across most North America, except for the far north. They might even stay put year-round in milder climates!
- Tree and Bush Paradise: House Finches love urban and suburban areas, farmlands, parks, and gardens with plenty of trees and bushes to explore.

Diet:

- Seed Samplers: These birds aren't picky eaters! They enjoy a variety of foods, including seeds, buds, flowers, leaves, and fruits. But they especially love sunflower seeds and berries.

Interesting Behaviors:

- Cheerful Chirps: House Finches are known for their happy, warbling songs.
- Feeder Acrobat: Watch them hang upside down or in any position as they munch on seeds at feeders. They're super acrobatic!
- Flocking Fun: These social birds often feed in groups and hop around in bushes together.

Fun Facts:

- <u>West to East Travelers</u>: House Finches were originally western birds, but in the 1940s, they hitched a ride east and are now found all over North America.
- <u>Red Means Ready</u>: The red color of male House Finches comes from their food. The brighter the red, the healthier the bird!
- <u>Songbird Duets</u>: Both male and female House Finches sing, making them one of the few bird species with duets!

Backyard Buddies:

- <u>Feeder Frenzy</u>: Attract them with foods in your feeders: tiny black-oil sunflower seeds, Nyjer seeds, mixed birdseed, peanuts, fruit, suet, and even sugar water.
- <u>Birdbath Bonanza</u>: Offer a shallow (1-3 inch deep) birdbath for them to drink and keep clean.
- <u>Feeling Safe is Key</u>: Place feeders near shrubs or trees to make them feel secure and encourage visits.
- <u>Birdhouse Bonanza (Optional)</u>: You can mount a birdhouse on a post in the middle of your yard, away from trees and buildings, to see if they want to raise a family.
- <u>Bushy Delights</u>: Planting shrubs near the ground can attract them, as they like to eat there.
- <u>Wreath Surprise</u>: Hanging a wreath on your door can also be a fun way to attract House Finches.

RECORD YOUR SIGHTINGS!

- Date: _____
- Location: _____
- What was the cardinal doing?: _____
_____
- Any exciting notes or observations?: _____
_____

(2) Black-capped Chickadee (Poecile atricapillus)

Size and Appearance:

- Little Ball of Personality: Black-capped Chickadees are small, with a cute black "cap and bib" outfit, white cheeks, and a soft gray back. They're easy to spot with their bold markings!

Habitat Preferences:

- Forest Friends, Backyard Buddies: Found across most of North America, they love mixed forests. But you can also see them in parks, gardens, and even at your feeders!

Black-capped Chickadee

Diet:

- Seed Stashers: Chickadees aren't picky eaters! They enjoy insects, seeds, and nuts. In winter, they especially love sunflower seeds, peanuts, and suet.

Interesting Behaviors:

- Curious and Chatty: These friendly birds love to explore and are very vocal. Their signature "chick-a-dee-dee-dee" call is their way of talking to each other.
- Super Squirrel Memory: Chickadees can remember where they hid food for up to a month – like tiny nature ninjas!
- Cool Winter Trick: They lower their body temperature at night to save energy in the cold – like a living sleep saver!

Fun Facts:

- Their Name Says It All: Their call sounds like "chick-a-dee-dee-dee," so that's how they got their name!
- Upside Down Munchers: They can hang upside down from branches to reach yummy snacks – like tiny acrobats!
- Bold and Brave: If you're patient, these chickadees might even take a seed right from your hand!

Fun Facts:

- <u>Their Name Says It All</u>: Their call sounds like "chick-a-dee-dee-dee," so that's how they got their name!
- <u>Upside Down Munchers</u>: They can hang upside down from branches to reach yummy snacks – like tiny acrobats!
- <u>Bold and Brave:</u> If you're patient, these chickadees might even take a seed right from your hand!

Bird Bath

Backyard Buddies:

- <u>Feeder Frenzy</u>: Attract them with peanuts, sunflower seeds, and suet in feeders. They like small, moving feeders or window feeders.
- <u>Nest Box Neighborhood</u>: Put up nest boxes in quiet areas of your yard. They like using them to raise their families.
- <u>Plant a Tree, Attract a Chickadee</u>: Planting willow, alder, or birch trees gives them natural places to nest.
- <u>Birdbath Bonanza</u>: Offer a shallow birdbath with rocks for perching. Dripping water can also attract them.
- <u>Listen Up!</u>: Learn their "chick-a-dee-dee-dee" call and listen for them in your yard. They might even respond to a "pishing" sound like a secret birdwatcher handshake!

Feeder

RECORD YOUR SIGHTINGS!

- Date: _____
- Location: _____
- What was the cardinal doing?: _____
_____
- Any exciting notes or observations?: _____
_____

(3) American Robin (Turdus migratorius)

Size and Appearance:

American Robin

- <u>Early Bird, Big Voice</u>: American Robins are more significant than most songbirds. They have a gray-brown body, an orange breast, and a dark head. Males have a bolder look, with black streaks on their throats.

Habitat Preferences:

- <u>Open Country Explorer</u>: You can find them almost anywhere in North America (except way up north). They love open spaces like woodlands, fields, and even your backyard!

Diet:
- <u>Worm Wrestling Champion:</u> These birds are super at catching earthworms for breakfast and dinner. In winter, they switch to a fruity feast of berries.

Interesting Behaviors:

- <u>Music in the Morning</u>: Robins are famous for their beautiful songs, especially early morning. They're like the natural world's alarm clock!
- <u>Winter Flock Party:</u> Come winter, robins love to hang out in big groups, especially near trees with berries.

Fun Facts:

- Early Risers Get the Worm: Because they sing at dawn, Robins are nicknamed "early birds" – for good reason! They know the best time to catch yummy worms is before anyone else wakes up.
- Superworm Vacuum Cleaners: These birds can eat up to 14 feet of earthworms in a single day – that's a lot of wiggly snacks!
- Sharp Eyes for Dinner: Robins have fantastic eyesight and can spot worms even if they hide underground!
- Springtime Singers: Their cheerful songs signify that spring is finally here!
- Long-Life Champions: Some Robins can live up to 14 years old in the wild – that's a long time for singing and catching worms!

Backyard Buddies:

- Feeder Frenzy: Attract them with mealworms, suet, and fruits in your feeders.
- Nest Box Neighbors: Put up nesting boxes before spring to give them a cozy place to raise their families.
- Winter Watch: During the winter, look for flocks of Robins in trees, especially near ones with berries.
- Skip the Sprays: Avoid using pesticides in your garden. This will attract more insects for Robins to eat and keep them happy!

RECORD YOUR SIGHTINGS!

- Date: _____
- Location: _____
- What was the cardinal doing?: _____ _____
- Any exciting notes or observations?: _____ _____

(4) Dark-eyed Junco (Junco hyemalis)

Size and Appearance:

- Gray Ghost with a Wink: Dark-eyed Juncos are small, sparrow-like birds with a gray hood, white belly, and a secret weapon - a bright white tail that flashes when they fly!

By IceuImgflip - Own work, CC BY-SA 4.0, https://commons.wikimedia.org/w/index.php?curid=146615895

Habitat Hoppers:
- Summer in the Forest, Winter in Your Backyard: Look for them in cool forests in summer. Then, when it snows, they magically appear in parks and backyards—like tiny winter messengers!

Diet:
- Ground Grub Hunters: Juncos love to hop on the ground searching for seeds and grains, especially in winter. In summer, they add insects and berries to their menu.

Interesting Behaviors:
- Cheery Tweeters, Winter Flockers: These birds have happy chirps and love to hang out in groups, especially during winter. It's like a snowball party for Juncos!
- Flashy Danger Signal: Watch for their white tails to flash – that's their way of warning other Juncos about danger!

Backyard Buddies:
- Ground Grub Feast: Attract them with seeds scattered on the ground or on a low feeder.
- Watery Oasis (Winter): In the cold months, offer a shallow, heated birdbath from which they can drink.
- Brushy Hideaway: Leave bushes untrimmed for them to hide in and feel safe.
- Berry Bonanza: Plant berry bushes for a natural Junco treat!

RECORD YOUR SIGHTINGS!

- Date: _____
- Location: _____
- What was the cardinal doing?: _____
- Any exciting notes or observations?: _____

(5) Song Sparrow (Melospiza melodia)

Size and Appearance:

- Secret Streaker: This sparrow is a master of disguise with brown and white streaks that blend into its surroundings. But listen closely, and its beautiful song will give it away!

Habitat Preferences:

- Backyard Buddy: Found all over North America (except way north), Song Sparrows feel right at home in gardens, fields, and areas with lots of bushes.

Song Sparrow

By Rhododendrites - Own work, CC BY-SA 4.0, https://commons.wikimedia.org/w/index.php?curid=118193669

Diet:

- Feathered Foodies: These birds aren't picky eaters! They enjoy a tasty mix of seeds, insects, and fruits. In spring, they find yummy protein-rich snacks for their chicks.

Interesting Behaviors:

- Morning Music: Listen to their beautiful songs, especially early morning. Each male Song Sparrow has a unique tune, making them like tiny rock stars of the bird world!
- Ground Gourmets: Song Sparrows spend much time on the ground, scratching for seeds and insects to eat.

Fun Facts:

- Singers with Style: Song Sparrows are named for their amazing songs, and each male has his unique melody.
- Adaptable Amigos: These birds are flexible and can live in many habitats.
- Mimic Masters: Listen closely! Song Sparrows can even copy the calls of other birds.
- Widespread Wonders: They're one of North America's most common sparrow species.
- Fluttery Flirting: During mating season, male Song Sparrows impress females with a unique flying display.

Backyard Buddies:

- <u>Feeder Frenzy</u>: Attract Song Sparrows with various seeds, such as sunflower seeds, millet, and cracked corn, on platform feeders or scattered on the ground.
- <u>Birdbath Bonanza</u>: A shallow bird bath will attract Song Sparrows for drinking and bathing.
- <u>Bushy Hideaways</u>: Plant dense shrubs and bushes to provide Song Sparrows with cover and places to build their nests. You can avoid trimming these areas during the nesting season.
- <u>Native Plant Paradise</u>: Planting native plants that produce seeds and berries will give Song Sparrows a natural food source in your yard.

RECORD YOUR SIGHTINGS!

- Date: _____
- Location: _____
- What was the cardinal doing?: _____
  _____
- Any exciting notes or observations?: _____
  _____

Why do birds fly south in the winter?

Because it's too far to walk!

What do you get if you cross a bird with a magician?

A flying sorcerer!

Group 3: Woodpeckers

(1) Downy Woodpecker (Dryobates pubescens)

Downy Woodpecker

Size and Appearance:

- Little Drummer, Big Personality: At only 6-7 inches tall, Downy Woodpeckers are the smallest woodpeckers around. They have a black-and-white checkered back and a bright red dot on their head (for males only).

Habitat Preferences:

- Tree-top traveler: Found nearly everywhere in North America, tree-top travelers love forests, parks, and even your backyard—especially if there are dead trees for them to peck on.

Diet:

- Bug Buffet: Downy Woodpeckers love using their strong beaks to peck for yummy insects like beetles and ants. They also enjoy seeds, nuts, and berries.

Interesting Behaviors:

- Drum Solo in the Trees: Listen for their drumming – it's their way of talking to each other and finding food.
- Super Sticky Tongues: Their tongues are super long and sticky, perfect for catching insects hiding deep inside trees.
- Upside Down Munchers: These acrobats can hang upside down from branches to reach yummy snacks!

RECORD YOUR SIGHTINGS!

- Date: _____
- Location: _____
- What was the cardinal doing?: _____ _____
- Are there any exciting notes or observations?: _____ _____ _____

Fun Facts:

- Smallest Woodpecker, Biggest Appetite: Despite their size, they can peck up to 16 times per second – that's super fast!
- Built-in Filters: They have special nose feathers to keep wood chips out while they peck.

(2) Hairy Woodpecker (Leuconotopicus villosus)

Hairy Woodpecker

Photo by <a href="https://unsplash.com/@anishlk?utm_content=creditCopyText&utm_medium=referral&utm_source=unsplash">Anish Lakkapragada</a> on <a href="https://unsplash.com/photos/a-bird-sitting-on-a-wire-with-its-mouth-open-3ejEseg4TkE?utm_content=creditCopyText&utm_medium=referral&utm_source=unsplash">Unsplash</a>

Size and Appearance:

- Striped Superstar: Hairy Woodpeckers are bigger than robins, with bold black and white stripes and a red crest (for males only).
- Forest Flyers: Look for them in mature forests with tall trees – their favorite hangout!

Diet:

Bug Busters: Hairy Woodpeckers use their strong beaks to peck for yummy beetle larvae hidden under tree bark. They also enjoy ants, fruits, and nuts.

Interesting Behaviors:

- Drummers in the Wild: Listen for their loud drumming! It's their way of talking and finding food.
- Upside Down Acrobats: These birds can hang upside down from branches – like tiny gymnasts!
- Home Builders: Hairy Woodpeckers carve out their own homes in trees.

Fun Facts:

- Look-alike Challenge: Hairy woodpeckers can be tricky to tell apart from Downy Woodpeckers, but They are bigger and have longer bills.
- Drumming Champions: Their drumming can be heard far away – like a forest drum solo!
- Forest Protectors: By eating insects, they help keep the forest healthy.

RECORD YOUR SIGHTINGS!

- Date: _____
- Location: _____
- What was the cardinal doing?: _____ _____
- Are there any exciting notes or observations?: _____ _____ _____

(3) Northern Flicker (Colaptes auratus)

Size and Appearance:

- <u>Flickering Friend</u>: Northern Flickers are medium-large woodpeckers with brown bodies and black bars. Look for a red cap (males) and yellow/red flashes under their wings (depending on where they live).

Habitat:
- Forest Edges & Your Yard: These woodpeckers love open woodlands and forest edges, but if there are trees in your backyard, you might even see them!

Diet:

Northern Flicker
northern flicker or common flicker
(Colaptes auratus)

<u>Ground Grub Hunters</u>: Unlike most woodpeckers, Flickers love to eat ants and beetles they find on the ground, using their long tongues to slurp them up! They also enjoy fruits and seeds.

Interesting Behaviors:

- <u>Drummers & Diggers</u>: Listen for their loud drumming and watch them dig in the dirt for yummy treats. They're like the drummers and chefs of the bird world!
- <u>Talking with Wicks</u>: Their call sounds like "wick-a-wick-a-wick" – a particular woodpecker language!
- <u>Horizontal Hangers</u>: Funny fact – Flickers often perch sideways on branches, not up and down like other woodpeckers.

RECORD YOUR SIGHTINGS!

- Date: _____
- Location: _____
- What was the cardinal doing?:
  _____
  _____
- Are there any exciting notes or observations?: _____
  _____
  _____
  ___

Fun Facts:

- <u>Super Sticky Tongue</u>: Their tongue can reach up to 2 inches past their beak, perfect for catching sneaky ants!
- <u>Short-distance Travelers</u>: Flickers might fly south for winter, but not too far.
- <u>Sideways Sitters</u>: Unlike most woodpeckers, they prefer to perch sideways on branches.

(4) Red-bellied Woodpecker (Melanerpes carolinus)

Red-bellied Woodpecker

Size and Appearance:
- Secret Redhead (Almost): Red-bellied Woodpeckers are medium-sized with a bright red cap, black and white stripes, and a white belly (though the red belly can be hard to spot!).

Habitat:
- Forest & Backyard Buddy: Found in forests and woodlands, they also love backyards with big trees – like a woodpecker party!

Diet:
Bug Buffet & More: These woodpeckers enjoy a mix of insects, fruits, and nuts, and even sometimes grab spiders or lizards for a snack! They love to visit feeders for yummy suet and seeds too.
Interesting Behaviors:

- Drummers and stashers: Listen for their loud drumming and watch them store food in bark crevices— like tiny forest chefs!
- Sticky Tongue Surprise: Their long tongues are super sticky, perfect for grabbing insects hiding in nooks and crannies.
- Climbing Champions: These woodpeckers are acrobatic climbers, always zipping up and down trees.

Fun Facts:
- Strong Beak Power: Their strong beak acts like a chisel, helping them find food and make their homes in trees.
- Sticky Situation Solver: Long, sticky tongues help them snatch insects hiding in tiny spaces.

Backyard Tips:
- Feeder Frenzy: Attract Red-bellied Woodpeckers with suet, peanuts, and sunflower seeds. They also enjoy fruits like apples and oranges.
- Nest Box Neighbors: Put up nest boxes with a 2-inch hole for them to raise their young woodpecker family.
- Watery Oasis: Offer a birdbath with fresh water for them to drink and bathe in.
- Treehouse Paradise: Plant a variety of trees and shrubs for them to explore and find food. If it's safe, leave some dead trees for them to make their nests in.

RECORD YOUR SIGHTINGS!
- Date: _____
- Location:_____
- What was the cardinal doing?: _____ _____
- Are there any exciting notes or observations?:_____ _____ _____ ___

(5) Pileated Woodpecker (Dryocopus pileatus)

Size and Appearance:
- Secret Redhead (Almost): Pileated Woodpeckers are the most enormous woodpeckers in North America! Look for their black body, white stripes, and a bright red mohawk (crest) on their head. Males also have a red mustache!

Habitat:
- Forest Giants: They prefer old forests with large trees for nesting and finding food. You might also see them in parks with big trees.

Diet:
- Carpenter Ant Champions: These woodpeckers love using their strong beaks to dig for yummy carpenter ants and beetle larvae living inside dead trees. They also enjoy fruits, nuts, and berries.

Pileated Woodpecker

Image by Veronika Andrews from Pixabay

Interesting Behaviors:

- These woodpeckers create large, rectangular holes in trees while searching for insects. They have a distinctive, loud, and echoing call and can be heard drumming on trees to communicate.

Interesting Behaviors:
- Big Holes: Pileated Woodpeckers make big, square holes in trees to find insects – like tiny woodworker rectangles!
- Loud & Clear Calls: Listen to their loud drumming and hear their calls echoing through the forest. It's their way of talking to each other.

Fun Facts:
- Apartment Builders: The holes they make become homes for other birds and animals after they're done.
- Super Strong Beaks: Their strong beaks and neck muscles help them chisel into wood like super tools!
- Long-distance Drummers: Their drumming can be heard from far away, like a forest drum solo!

Backyard Tips:
- Feeder Frenzy: Attract Pileated Woodpeckers with suet, peanuts, and sunflower seeds.
- Natural Homes: If it's safe, leave large dead trees standing in your yard for them to nest in.
- Watery Oasis: Offer a birdbath with fresh water for them to drink and bathe in.
- Forest Protectors: Try to plant trees and preserve forests to give these amazing birds a home.

RECORD YOUR SIGHTINGS!

- Date: _____
- Location: _____
- What was the cardinal doing?: _____ _____
- Are there any exciting notes or observations?: _____ _____ _____ ___

Group 4: Water Birds

(1) Mallard Duck (Anas platyrhynchos)

Size and Appearance:

- **Drakes in Green Suits**: Male Mallard Ducks are colorful with shiny green heads, white collars, and brown chests.

- **Mottled Marvels**: Female Mallard Ducks are brown with bright orange bills and look slightly different from the males.

Habitat Preferences:

- **Pond Pals & Backyard Buddies:** Mallard Ducks are very adaptable and can live in ponds, lakes, rivers, and even your backyard pond if it's big enough!

Diet:

Dabbling Diners: Mallard Ducks are like underwater vacuum cleaners, tipping their bodies to eat plants, insects, and small fish. They also enjoy seeds and grains sometimes.

Interesting Behaviors:

- **Quacking Queens:** The loud "quack" you hear is usually the female Mallard Duck talking! Males make quieter sounds.
- **Partner Pals:** Mallard Ducks often find a mate in the fall and stick together until spring, when the female lays eggs.

Mallard Duck

Photo by Jason Leung on Unsplash

RECORD YOUR SIGHTINGS!

- Date: _____
- Location:_____
- What was the cardinal doing?: _____ _____
- Are there any exciting notes or observations?:_____ _____ _____

Fun Facts:

- **Secret Family History**: Believe it or not, most pet ducks you see are related to Mallard Ducks!
- **Speedy Swimmers**: These ducks can fly up to 55 miles per hour – that's fast for a bird with webbed feet!

Backyard Tips:

- **Feeder Fun**: Attract Mallard Ducks with a sprinkle of cracked corn, birdseed, or grains near the water's edge.
- **Nesting Needs**: Leave tall grass or reeds near the water for them to build their nests.
- **Watery Oasis:** Make sure there's a pond or a large birdbath for them to swim and drink in.
- **Planted Paradise:** Plant native plants around the water, providing them with cover and materials to build their nests.

(2) Great Blue Heron (Ardea herodias)

Size and Appearance:

- Tall & Blue: Towering nearly 4 feet tall, Great Blue Herons are giants with long legs, sharp yellow bills, and blue-gray feathers. Watch for their S-curved necks as they stand super still.

Habitat Preferences:

- Lake & Marsh Lookout: These herons love shallow waters like lakes, rivers, and marshes – perfect for hunting fish!

Diet:

Fishy Feasts: Fish are their favorite snack, but they enjoy frogs, small animals, and insects. They stand patiently and strike fast with their sharp beaks.

Interesting Behaviors:

- Solo Hunters, Colony Nesters: They hunt alone but live in big groups called rookeries to raise their young in tall nests.
- Slow & Steady Strikers: These herons move slowly and take off with their necks tucked in for a graceful flight.

Fun Facts:

- Day & Night Hunters: Great Blue Herons have fantastic vision and can catch food even at night!
- Big Swallowers: Their stretchy throats let them gulp down large prey whole!
- Lightweight Giants: Despite their size, they're light (like 5 pounds) thanks to hollow bones!

Great Blue Heron

RECORD YOUR SIGHTINGS!

- Date: _____
- Location:_____
- What was the cardinal doing?: _____ _____
- Are there any exciting notes or observations?:_____ _____ _____ ___

Backyard Tips:

- Fishy Feasts (for Large Ponds): If you have a large pond, keeping it well-stocked with fish might attract them.
- Nest High: Tall trees or nesting platforms near water can provide them a place to raise their families.
- Shallow Waters: A pond or water feature with shallow areas is ideal for them to wade and hunt.
- Planted Paradise: Planting native plants near water gives them cover and an excellent spot to find food.

(3) Canada Goose (Branta canadensis)

Canada Goose

Size and Appearance:

- Big with Bold Stripes: Canada Geese are large with black heads and necks, white cheek patches, and brown-gray bodies.

Habitat Preferences:

- Lake to Lawn Loungers: Adaptable geese! They can live in lakes, parks, and even on golf courses, as long as there's water and grass.

Diet:

Grass Gobblers & Grain Grazers: These geese mainly eat grass, plants, and seeds. They might also munch on your lawn!

Interesting Behaviors:

- Fly in a V & Make Friends: Look for their V-shaped flocks as they fly – it helps them save energy and stay together. They're social birds, too!
- Protective Parents: During the breeding season, they become super protective of their nests and goslings (baby geese).

Fun Facts:

- Mileage Masters: Canada Geese can fly long distances – up to 1,500 miles in a day!
- Honking Helpers: Their honking helps them communicate with each other, like a goose language!

Backyard Tips:

- Skip the Bread: While they may come for it, bread isn't healthy for geese. Offer them more nutritious options like grains or corn.
- Peaceful Coexistence: Respect their nests and avoid getting too close, especially with goslings.

RECORD YOUR SIGHTINGS!

- Date: _____
- Location: _____
- What was the cardinal doing?: _____ _____
- Are there any exciting notes or observations?: _____ _____ _____ ___

(4) American coot (Fulica americana)

Size and Appearance:

- <u>Medium-sized swimmer:</u> The American Coot is about the size of a duck. It has a slate-gray body, a white bill with a black tip, and bright red eyes.

Habitat Preferences:

- <u>Pond & Marsh Pals:</u> Look for them in freshwater areas like ponds, lakes, and marshes – they love plants!

American coot
Image by <u>Freddy</u> from <u>Pixabay</u>

Diet:

<u>Plant Divers:</u> These birds mainly eat plants and algae underwater but also enjoy small fish and insects sometimes.

Interesting Behaviors:

- <u>Great Swimmers</u>, Funny Flyers: American Coots are excellent swimmers but struggle to take off – they need a running start! They also bob their heads as they walk on land.
- <u>Loud & Protective</u>: Listen for their croaking calls and watch out – they can be aggressive when protecting their young.

RECORD YOUR SIGHTINGS!

- Date: _____
- Location: _____
- What was the cardinal doing?: _____ _____
- Are there any exciting notes or observations?: _____ _____ _____ ___

Fun Facts:
- <u>Not Really Ducks</u>: Although they look similar, American Coots are in a different bird family than ducks!

- <u>Nesting Tricks:</u> They build their nests to float on the water, making them safe from land predators.

Backyard Tips:

- <u>More Plants, Less Fuss:</u> Having a variety of aquatic plants in your pond or water feature will attract them naturally.

(5) Wood Duck (Aix sponsa)

Size and Appearance:

- <u>Males in Jewels:</u> Male Wood Ducks are the flashy ones, with bright green heads, red eyes, and a white bib. Females are brown with pretty eye rings and blue wing patches.

Habitat Preferences:

- <u>Wooded Waterfowl:</u> Wood Ducks like swampy forests with ponds and trees – perfect for swimming and perching!

Diet:

<u>Dabbling Divers:</u> They eat seeds, fruits, insects, and plants. They dabble at the water's surface for food and can sometimes dive to get a snack.

Interesting Behaviors:

- <u>Treetop Nest Jumpers:</u> Wood Ducks nest in tree holes – and their ducklings jump out as soon as they hatch! Don't worry, they're tough!
- <u>Fast & Feathery Flyers:</u> These ducks are surprisingly strong fliers, zipping and zagging through the air.

Wood Duck

Image by <u>Michel Rohan</u> from <u>Pixabay</u>

RECORD YOUR SIGHTINGS!

- Date: _____
- Location: _____
- What was the cardinal doing?: _____ _____
- Are there any exciting notes or observations?: _____ _____ _____ ___

Fun Facts:

- <u>Clawed Climbers</u>: Wood Ducks have special claws on their feet to grip onto tree branches!
- <u>High-Rise Homes</u>: Unlike most ducks, they nest in holes high up in trees.
- <u>Drab Dudes in Disguise</u>: Male Wood Ducks lose their fancy feathers after mating season and look more like females for a while.

<u>Backyard Tips:</u>

- <u>Feathered Foodies:</u> Attract Wood Ducks with corn, nuts, and fruits near water.
- <u>Treetop Apartments:</u> Put up nest boxes on trees near water for them to raise their young.
- <u>Watery Oasis:</u> Make sure there's a pond or water feature with plants for them to explore.
- <u>Planted Paradise:</u> Plant trees and shrubs around the water, giving them cover and resting places.

Group 5: Birds of Prey

(1) Red-tailed Hawk (Buteo jamaicensis)

Red-tailed Hawk
Image by sondinh2000 from Pixabay

Size and Appearance:

- **Big with a Bold Tail**: Red-tailed Hawks are large birds with broad wings and a bright red tail (their giveaway!). Their body color varies, but they often have a light chest and dark belly band.

Habitat Preferences:

- **Forest to City Flyer**: Adaptable Hawks! They can live in forests, grasslands, deserts, and even cities – as long as there's space to hunt and tall trees to nest.

Diet:

- **Mouse Munchers & More**: These hawks mainly eat small animals like mice, rats, and rabbits. They also enjoy birds, snakes, and sometimes insects – catching them by surprise from high up!

Interesting Behaviors:

- **Soaring Circles & Screaming Calls**: Watch them soar in circles with fantastic eyesight, searching for food. Listen to their high-pitched scream, a famous hawk sound in movies!
- **High-Rise Homes**: They build big nests in tall trees or on cliffs, adding to them every year.

Fun Facts:

- **Hollywood Hawk Scream:** That scary screech in movies? It's probably a Red-tailed Hawk!
- **Super Sight:** Their vision is incredible – they can see a mouse from way up in the sky!
- **Tail Tale:** Baby Red-tailed Hawks don't get red tails until they're about a year old.

RECORD YOUR SIGHTINGS!

- Date: _____
- Location: _____
- What was the cardinal doing?: _____
- Are there any exciting notes or observations?: _____

Backyard Tips:

- **Natural Hunters**: Hawks mostly hunt for food in wild areas. Keeping your yard healthy can help the small animals they eat, which in turn helps the hawk population.
- **Nest Respect**: If you see a hawk nest in a tall tree, leave them alone to raise their young.
- **Watery Oasis**: A clean birdbath with water is lovely for them to drink, although they find most water in nature.
- **Tree haven**: Keeping various trees in your yard gives them places to perch and look out for prey.

(2) American Kestrel (Falco sparverius)

Size and Appearance:

- **Little & Loud**: American Kestrels are the smallest falcons in North America, about the size of a robin! Males have a blue head and rusty back, while females are mostly brown.

Habitat Preferences:

- **Open & Up High**: They love open areas like grasslands, meadows, and even deserts, which are perfect for hunting from high perches.

Diet:

- **Insect Inhalers**: These Kestrels are bug-eating champions! They love grasshoppers, beetles, and other insects they swoop down to catch.

Interesting Behaviors:

- **Family Hunting Fun**: Young Kestrels sometimes hunt with their parents to practice their skills. Watch for them flying together!
- **The Kestrel Kluck**: Listen for their high-pitched "klee klee" calls – it's their way of talking.

American Kestrel
Image by Kev from Pixabay

RECORD YOUR SIGHTINGS!

- Date: _____
- Location: _____
- What was the cardinal doing?: _____ _____
- Are there any exciting notes or observations?: _____ _____ _____

Fun Facts:

- **Fast & Furious**: American Kestrels can hover mid-air while hunting, thanks to their quick wing beats.
- **Feathered Fashionistas**: Males and females have different colored feathers – uncommon for birds!
- **Recycled Homes**: Kestrels don't build their nests – they often take over old woodpecker holes or nest boxes.

Backyard Tips:

- **Snack Station**: Attract Kestrels with a bird feeder filled with suet or seeds (in moderation).
- **Home Sweet Nest Box**: Put a nest box in your yard to give them a place to raise their young.
- **Keep it Open**: If you have open areas in your yard with short grass or dead snags, they might be attracted to them for hunting.

(3) Great Horned Owl (Bubo virginianus)

Size and Appearance:

- <u>Big with Feathery Horns</u>: Great Horned Owls are large with tufts of feathers resembling horns on their heads. They have mottled brown feathers, yellow eyes, and a white bib.

Habitat Preferences:

- <u>Forest to City Fun</u>: Adaptable owls! They can live in forests, deserts, and even cities – as long as there's a mix of open space to hunt and trees to hide.

Diet:

- <u>Nighttime Nibblers:</u> These owls are strong hunters and eat all sorts of animals at night, from rabbits and squirrels to other birds and insects! They use their excellent vision and hearing to find prey.

Interesting Behaviors:

- <u>Hooting Heroes</u>: Listen for their deep hoots that can travel far. They also hoot to defend their territory and talk to each other.
- <u>Super Swivel Heads</u>: Great Horned Owls can turn their heads almost all the way around – that's 270 degrees!

Great Horned Owl
Image by <u>Amber Dawn</u> from <u>Pixabay</u>

RECORD YOUR SIGHTINGS!

- Date: _____
- Location:_____
- What was the cardinal doing?: _____ _____
- Are there any exciting notes or observations?:_____ _____ _____

Fun Facts:

- <u>Super Strong Grip</u>: Their grip is firm enough to squeeze a prey's spine!
- <u>Striped Surprise</u>: Sometimes, they're called "tiger owls" because of their striped feathers.
- <u>Borrowed Homes</u>: These owls don't build their nests – they often take over old nests or use holes in trees and cliffs.

Backyard Tips:

- <u>Natural Helpers</u>: The best way to help them is to keep your yard healthy, so it has many small animals for them to eat.
- <u>Owl Apartments</u>: You can leave large trees to provide them with a place to live or put up special nesting platforms.
- <u>Night Light Nuisance</u>: Try to keep outdoor lights low. Bright lights can bother them when they hunt at night.

(4) Barn Owl (Tyto alba)

Size and Appearance:

- Heart-Shaped Head Hero: Barn Owls are medium-sized with a white, heart-shaped face, dark eyes, and golden-brown wings.

Habitat Preferences:

- Farms & Fields: They like open areas like farms, grasslands, and prairies – perfect for hunting with less clutter. Old barns are their favorite homes!

Diet:

- Midnight Mouse Munchers: These owls hunt mainly small animals like mice and voles at night. Their fantastic hearing and vision in the dark make them super sneaky hunters!

Interesting Behaviors:

- Silent Swoopers: Barn Owls fly silently to catch their prey by surprise – no noisy flapping! They also have a spooky screech instead of a hoot.
- Daytime Dozers & Nighttime Nibblers: Look for them roosting in barns or trees during the day. At night, they're out hunting!

Barn Owl
Image by Amber Dawn from Pixabay

RECORD YOUR SIGHTINGS!

- Date: _____
- Location:_____
- What was the cardinal doing?:
  _____
  _____
- Are there any exciting notes or observations?:_____
  _____
  _____

Fun Facts:

- Hear Here! Barn Owls can hunt in total darkness because their hearing is incredible.
- Pellet Power: They swallow their prey whole and spit up leftover fur and bones in a pellet ball.
- Rodent Regulators: A Barn Owl family can eat over 1,000 mice in a summer – they're natural pest control!

Backyard Tips:

- Happy Hunting Grounds: Keeping your yard healthy with many small animals helps attract them (indirectly).
- Barn Owl BnBs: Put special nest boxes in quiet, dark areas like barns or tall trees. Could you make sure the entrance is clear for easy access?
- Watery Oasis: A natural water source like a pond or birdbath helps the small animals they eat.
- Safe Havens: Leave old barns and tree cavities undisturbed – they might be a Barn Owl's home!
-

(5) Bald Eagle (Haliaeetus leucocephalus)

Size and Appearance:

- Big with a Bold Look: Bald Eagles are large birds with a brown body, white head and tail, and a bright yellow beak and feet – easy to spot!

Habitat Preferences:

- Lakes & Coasts: They prefer areas near large bodies of water like lakes, rivers, and coasts, perfect for fishing and finding tall trees to nest in.

Bald Eagle

Diet:

- Fishy Feasts: Bald Eagles love fish, which they catch with their sharp talons. They might also eat birds, small animals, or leftover dead animals. Sometimes, they steal fish from other birds!

Interesting Behaviors:

- Soaring Stars & Big Builders: They fly high and strong and build huge nests called eyries in tall trees or on cliffs. These nests can get enormous over time!
- Lifelong Lovers & Show-Offs: Bald Eagles find a mate for life and put on fantastic flying shows to impress each other.

RECORD YOUR SIGHTINGS!

- Date: _____
- Location: _____
- What was the cardinal doing?: _____ _____
- Are there any exciting notes or observations?: _____ _____ _____ _____

Fun Facts:

- Super Sight: They can see fish in the water from way up in the sky!
- Giant Homes: Their nests can be the biggest of any bird in North America!
- Not Bald: Believe it or not, "bald" meant "white" – they're not bald!
- Back from the Brink: Bald Eagles were almost extinct due to pollution, but they return thanks to protection!

Backyard Tips:

- Healthy Waters, Happy Eagles: Keeping lakes and rivers healthy with lots of fish helps them find food (indirectly).
- Big Tree Homes: Leaving large trees near water lets them build their giant nests. Don't bother them while they're raising young!
- Clean Water Counts: Clean lakes, rivers, and ponds are essential for the fish they eat.
- Peaceful Place to Perch: Protecting trees and natural areas gives them places to rest and look out for prey.

Group 6: Ground Feeders

(1) Northern Bobwhite (Colinus virginianus)

Northern Bobwhite
Image by Vantha So from Pixabay

Size and Appearance:

- Small & Round with Stripes: Bobwhites are small, plump birds. Males have brown bodies, black caps, and white stripes on their faces and throat. Females are browner with buff stripes.

Habitat Preferences:

- Fields and Meadows: They like open areas with tall grass, shrubs, and scattered trees, perfect for finding food and hiding from danger.

Diet:

- Seed Savvy & Insect Snacker: Bobwhites eat primarily seeds and grains found on the ground, along with some insects, as snacks.

Interesting Behaviors:

- The Bob-WHITE Call: Listen for their loud "bob-WHITE!" call – it's their way of talking and marking territory.
- Ground Gangs: Bobwhites are social and hang out in small groups called coveys, looking for food together.

RECORD YOUR SIGHTINGS!

- Date: _____
- Location: _____
- What was the cardinal doing?: _____
- Are there any exciting notes or observations?: _____

Fun Facts:

- Speedy & Sneaky: They can run fast and have great camouflage to avoid getting eaten!
- Bob-Named for their Call: Their name comes right from their loud "bob-WHITE!" call.
- Seed Spreaders: Bobwhites help plants grow in new places by eating and dropping seeds.
- Short & Sweet Life: Sadly, most Bobwhites only live for a year or two.
- Busy Breeders: They can raise several clutches of chicks in one summer!

Backyard Tips:

- Ground Grub Station: Scatter seeds and grains on the ground for them to eat. Plant native grasses and shrubs that grow seeds they like.
- Brushy Homes: Leave piles of branches and tall grass for them to hide and nest in. Don't disturb their nests in spring and summer.
- Watery Oasis: A small birdbath or pond helps them stay calm and clean.
- Shrub Shelter: Planting bushes and making brush piles gives them safe places to rest and hide. By keeping your yard diverse with a mix of plants, you can help them thrive.

(2) Eastern Towhee (Pipilo erythrophthalmus)

Size and Appearance:

- **Medium with Bold Colors:** Eastern Towhees are a bit bigger than robins. Males are dramatic—black and white with rusty orange sides. Females are brown instead of black but still have the orange.

Habitat Preferences:

- **Brushy Borders & Forest Floors:** They love areas with thick bushes and ground cover, such as forest edges, overgrown fields, or dense woodlands.

Diet:

- **Seed Savvy & Berry Buffets:** Eastern Towhees eat various things—seeds, fruits, berries, and insects. Like tiny dancers, they scratch through leaves on the ground with both feet to find yummy things to eat.

Interesting Behaviors:

- **The "Drink-Your-Tea!" Song:** Listen for their funny call that sounds like "Drink your tea!"
- **Hidden Nest Builders:** They build cup-shaped nests low in bushes or even on the ground, hidden well in thick plants.

Fun Facts:

- **Secret Scratch:** Their two-footed hopping scratch is unique – you won't see many birds forage like that!
- **SWinter Wanderers:** Northern populations of Eastern Towhees migrate south for the winter, while their southern cousins stay put year-round.

Backyard Tips:

- **Brushy Bonanza:** Leaving areas of your yard with overgrown shrubs and brush piles can provide them with hiding spots and nesting sites.
- **Leaf Litter Buffet:** A layer of fallen leaves on the ground can attract insects and worms – a tasty Eastern Towhee snack!
- **Seed Symphony:** Scattering seeds like sunflower chips or millet on the ground can attract them to your yard for a delicious meal (but avoid feeders as they prefer natural foraging).

Eastern Towhee
Image by Miles Moody from Pixabay

RECORD YOUR SIGHTINGS!

- Date: _____
- Location: _____
- What was the cardinal doing?: _____
- Are there any exciting notes or observations?: _____

(3) Wild Turkey (Meleagris gallopavo)

Size and Appearance:

- Big & Bold: Wild Turkeys are large! Males (toms) are like walking rainbows with a fan-shaped tail and a bright red head. Females (hens) are smaller and browner.

Wild Turkey

Habitat Preferences:

- Forest Feasting: They love mixed forests with open areas for hiding and finding food. Grasslands and swamps are sometimes their home, too. Trees are for sleeping, and open space is for eating!

Diet:

- Acorns to Ants: Wild Turkeys are like forest vacuum cleaners, eating acorns, nuts, seeds, berries, insects, and even tiny frogs! They scratch through leaves to find yummy things on the ground.

Interesting Behaviors:
- Gobble Gobble Talk: Listen for the loud gobble of the males – it's how they show off and attract mates. At night, they sleep high up in trees and can actually fly short distances!

RECORD YOUR SIGHTINGS!

- Date: _____
- Location:_____
- What was the cardinal doing?: _____
- Are there any exciting notes or observations?:_____

Fun Facts:

- Super Senses: They see and hear well, making them challenging to sneak up on!
- Fast on Foot & Feathered Flight: Wild Turkeys can run fast and even fly short bursts at high speeds!
- Almost an Eagle: Benjamin Franklin wanted the Wild Turkey to be our national bird, not the Bald Eagle!
- Talkative Turkeys: They have a whole vocabulary of over 20 sounds to communicate with each other.

Backyard Tips:

- Turkey Treats: Scatter corn, seeds, and nuts on the ground for them to eat. Plant bushes with berries and trees with nuts to attract them naturally.
- Brushy Homes: Leave areas with tall grass and brush piles for them to nest in. They build simple nests on the ground hidden in thick plants.
- Watery Oasis: A small birdbath or pond helps them stay cool and clean.

(4) Killdeer (Charadrius vociferus)

Size and Appearance:

- <u>Size & Appearance:</u> Medium shorebird (9-11 inches), brown back, white belly, two black chest bands. White forehead, black facial mask, red-orange eyes.

Habitat Preferences:

- <u>Habitat:</u> Adaptable, prefers open areas with gravel or sand. Found on shores, fields, even parking lots and rooftops.

Diet:

- Insects (beetles, grasshoppers), spiders, worms, and occasionally seeds or small vertebrates.

Interesting Behaviors:

- Known for "broken-wing" display to distract predators from well-camouflaged nests on gravel or sand.

Fun Facts:

- Named for their loud "kill-deer" call.
- Feign injury to protect young.
- Excellent runners, forage by darting across the ground.

Backyard Tips:

- Food: Leave bare ground/gravel for insect foraging.
- Nesting: Maintain gravel/sand patches or short grass (avoid disturbance during breeding season).
- Water: Provide a shallow birdbath or natural puddle.
- Shelter: Keep pets/predators away from nests—plant native grasses for cover and foraging.
- Space: Leave open areas for running and foraging (prefer large, open spaces with minimal human disturbance).

Killdeer

Image by Roaming Owls.com from Pixabay

RECORD YOUR SIGHTINGS!

- Date: _____
- Location: _____
- What was the cardinal doing?: _____ _____
- Are there any exciting notes or observations?: _____ _____ _____

(5) Mourning Dove (Zenaida macroura)

Size and Appearance:

- Medium-sized bird (9-13 inches) with a long, pointed tail.
- Soft, grayish-brown plumage with black wing spots.
- Small, black beak and pinkish legs.

Habitat Preferences:

- Adaptable, prefers open areas (fields, parks, gardens) and perches on wires.

Diet:

- Almost entirely seeds (grasses, weeds, grains).
- Occasionally, snails or insects.

Interesting Behaviors:

- Gentle cooing call ("coo-oo, coo, coo, coo").
- Fast, agile flight with whistling wings during takeoff/landing.
- Builds flimsy nests (trees, shrubs, ledges) with 2 white eggs.
- Drinks without lifting head.
- Prolific breeders (up to 6 broods per year).
- "Gular fluttering" - rapid throat vibration to cool down.
- Heavily hunted, but the population remains stable due to high reproduction.

Backyard Tips:

- Food: Ground/platform feeder with millet, cracked corn, and sunflower seeds.
- Nesting: Nesting platforms, dense shrubs/trees (sheltered with visibility).
- Water: Shallow birdbath with a steady water source.
- Shelter: Native shrubs/trees for cover and perching (avoid disturbing nests).
- Space: Open area for ground foraging. Avoid pesticides harming their food.

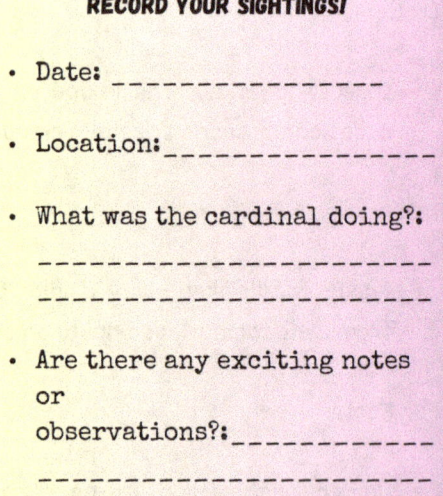

Mourning Dove

Image by Jack Bulmer from Pixabay

RECORD YOUR SIGHTINGS!

- Date: _____
- Location: _____
- What was the cardinal doing?: _____ _____
- Are there any exciting notes or observations?: _____ _____ _____

Image by Stewart Gunn from Pixabay

Group 7: Singing Birds

(1) Northern Mockingbird (Mimus polyglottos)

Size and Appearance:

- Medium songbird (8-11 inches) with long tail.
- Gray back, white belly, long legs, white wing patches.

Habitat Preferences:

- Adaptable (urban/suburban areas, parks, gardens, fields).
- Needs dense shrubs/trees for nesting and open areas for foraging.

Northern Mockingbird

Photo by Nathan Rostampour: https://www.pexels.com/photo/close-up-shot-of-a-northern-mockingbird-10960922/

Diet:

- Omnivorous: insects (summer), fruits/berries (winter).

Interesting Behaviors:

- Mimics up to 200 sounds (other birds, dogs barking, etc.).
- Sings day/night (especially breeding season).
- Defends nesting areas fiercely.
-

RECORD YOUR SIGHTINGS!

- Date: _____
- Location:_____
- What was the cardinal doing?: _____ _____
- Are there any exciting notes or observations?:_____ _____ _____

Fun Facts:

- Excellent memory, remembers threats.
- Featured in "To Kill a Mockingbird."
- Group called a "mimicry" (or "mockery").

Backyard Tips:

- Food: Fruit trees (mulberry, elderberry), mealworms, suet, and raisins.
- Nesting: Dense shrubs/trees (thorny like holly, hawthorn preferred).
- Water: Birdbath with fresh water in the open area.
- Shelter: Native plants for cover and perching (avoid pesticides).
- Space: Open areas for foraging/singing (vantage points for viewing).

(2) House Wren (Troglodytes aedon)

Size and Appearance:

- Small & Songful: House Wrens are robin-sized with a plump body and a perky tail they hold high. There is no white eyebrow stripe here, which helps tell them apart from other wrens.

Habitat Preferences:

- Backyard Buddies: House Wrens are all over North and South America, from Canada to the tip! They like many places with shrubs and brush to hide in, including gardens, parks, forests, and even your backyard!

House Wren

Photo by Daniel Shapiro: https://www.pexels.com/photo/house-wren-bird-16881501/

Diet:

- Insect-Eating Extraordinaire: These little birds are insectivores, meaning they mostly eat insects and spiders. They hunt all around, on the ground, in bushes, and even on tree bark, helping to keep your garden pest-free!

Interesting Behaviors:

- Busy & Bold: House Wrens are full of energy and always curious. They love to sing – listen for their bubbly, happy song! Males are especially busy in spring, building many pretend nests to impress the females.

RECORD YOUR SIGHTINGS!

- Date: _____
- Location: _____
- What was the cardinal doing?: _____ _____
- Are there any exciting notes or observations?: _____ _____ _____

Fun Facts:

- Little But Lionhearted: Don't let their size fool you – House Wrens are brave and will fight much bigger birds to protect their nest!
- Cozy Cave Dwellers: These tiny birds can fit in surprisingly small places – sometimes, they even nest in old shoes, cans, or mailboxes!
- Big Voice, Tiny Body: Their songs are loud and complicated, even though they're little birds. You can hear them from far away!

Backyard Tips:

- Bug Buffet & Brushy Shelter: Skip pesticides to create a tasty insect feast for wrens, and pile up branches to hide in and find more snacks!
- Nest Box Bonanza & Watery Oasis: Put up a nest box early in spring for a potential wren home in a quiet area, and add a shallow birdbath to keep them cool and clean.

(3) Gray Catbird (Dumetella carolinensis)

Size and Appearance:

- Gray & Sleek: Gray Catbirds are medium-sized with a relaxed all-gray body, a black cap, and a long black tail with a hidden red surprise underneath.

Habitat Preferences:

- Brushy Backyards: They love hiding in dense thickets, shrubs, and gardens – anywhere with lots of cover for their nest and yummy food.

Diet:

- Bug Buffet & Berry Bonanza: Gray Catbirds eat a mix of things – insects, spiders, fruits, and berries. They focus on bugs in summer, while fall and winter are all about juicy fruits.

Interesting Behaviors:

- Master Mimicker: Listen for their funny cat-like "mew" meow! They can also copy other birds and even weird sounds like car alarms.
- Secret Nest Builders: They build their nests well-hidden in thick bushes, making them hard to find.

Gray Catbird
Photo by Jack Bulmer: https://www.pexels.com/photo/a-close-up-shot-of-a-gray-catbird-8169912/

RECORD YOUR SIGHTINGS!

- Date: _____
- Location: _____
- What was the cardinal doing?: _____ _____
- Are there any exciting notes or observations?: _____ _____ _____

Fun Facts:

- Songbird Superstar: Gray Catbirds have a massive song repertoire with over 100 different tunes!
- Night Navigators: These clever birds migrate at night, using the stars to guide their way.
- One-Shot Molt: Unlike most birds, Gray Catbirds lose all their feathers at once, like a whole new outfit!

Backyard Tips:

- Berry Bushes & Birdbath Bonanza: Plant berry bushes that they love, and set up a birdbath with fresh water for them to cool off and splash around.
- Feeder Frenzy & Brushy Hideaways: Hang a feeder with suet and mealworms for a tasty treat. Leave areas of your yard with thick shrubs and bushes for them to build their nests and feel safe.
- Skip the Sprays: Avoid pesticides so they have plenty of insects to eat.

(4) Eastern Meadowlark (Sturnella magna)

Size and Appearance:

- <u>Bold & Beautiful</u>: Eastern Meadowlarks are medium-sized with bright yellow bellies and a black "V" for victory on their chest. Their brown backs with streaks help them hide in tall grass.

Habitat Preferences:

- <u>Grassland Gang</u>: They love wide-open spaces like meadows, prairies, and even grassy roadsides. Lots of ground cover is a must for hiding their nests and finding yummy food.

Diet:

- <u>Insect Eater & Seed Savvy</u>: These birds mostly eat insects in summer but switch to seeds and grains in winter when bugs are scarce.

Interesting Behaviors:

- <u>Melodies in the Meadow</u>: Listen for their lovely songs – they sing from high spots like fence posts to attract mates and claim territory. Meadowlarks build their nests hidden in the grass on the ground.

Eastern Meadowlark

RECORD YOUR SIGHTINGS!

- Date: _____
- Location: _____
- What was the cardinal doing?: _____ _____
- Are there any exciting notes or observations?: _____ _____ _____

Fun Facts:

- <u>Songbird Superstar</u>: Eastern Meadowlarks have a whole collection of songs, some with clear whistling notes!
- <u>Hidden Homes</u>: They're camouflage champions, making their nests hard to find.
- <u>Speedy on the Ground</u>: When threatened, they often run rather than fly, relying on good hiding skills.
- <u>Flash & Glide</u>: Their flight style is unique. They beat their wings quickly and coast for short distances.
- <u>Bright Warning</u>: Their yellow bellies tell predators they're not easy to catch!

Backyard Tips:

- <u>Seed Symphony & Watery Oasis</u>: Scatter seeds and offer mealworms for a tasty treat. A birdbath or small pond is a great way to keep them cool and clean.
- <u>Grassy Getaways</u>: Leave some areas of your yard with tall grass for them to hide and nest in. You can avoid mowing during nesting season.
- <u>Natural Neighbors</u>: Plant native grasses and wildflowers to create a meadow feel. Skip the pesticides so there are plenty of insects to eat.

(5) Wood Thrush (Hylocichla mustelina)

Size and Appearance:

- Spotted & Songful: Wood Thrushes are medium-sized with a reddish-brown back and a white belly with dark spots. Their big eyes and round body make them easy to recognize.

Habitat Preferences:

- Forest Friends: They love cool, damp woods with many trees and bushes close to the ground, especially near streams and swamps. Significant areas of forest are essential for their survival.

Diet:

- Insect Eater & Berry Bonanza: Wood Thrushes mainly eat insects in spring and summer, but they also love fruits and berries in fall when bugs are harder to find.

Interesting Behaviors:

- Melody Maker: Listen for their lovely flute-like songs echoing through the forest – they sing from hidden spots in the trees! They like to search for food on the ground, kicking through leaves with their strong legs. Their nests are cup-shaped and built in the branches of trees, sometimes with mud added for extra strength.

Fun Facts:

- Songbird Superstar: Wood Thrushes are famous for their outstanding, magical songs, which can be heard throughout the forest.
- Leaf Flippers have an incredible way of finding food. They use their beaks to flip over leaves, uncovering yummy insects hiding underneath!
- Travel Champs: Wood Thrushes are long-distance travelers. In the winter, they fly from North America to Central America.

Backyard Tips:

- Yummy Treats & Watery Oasis: To attract them, put out mealworms, suet, and berries.
- Forest Feeling: If you have a yard with big trees and bushes, leave them alone! You can even add a birdbath or small pond for fresh water.
- Leaf Litter & Natural Shelter: Plant various native trees and bushes to create a thick area under the trees. Let fallen leaves pile up on the ground – that's where they find their food!

Wood Thrush (Photo Credit Pixabay)

RECORD YOUR SIGHTINGS!

- Date: _____
- Location:_____
- What was the cardinal doing?: _____ _____
- Are there any exciting notes or observations?:_____ _____ _____

70

Group 8: Seasonal Visitors

(1) Ruby-throated Hummingbird (Archilochus colubris)

Size and Appearance:

- <u>Tiny & Glittering</u>: Ruby-throated Hummingbirds are the tiniest birds in North America! Males have flashy red throats, while males and females have shimmering green backs and white bellies. Their beaks are thin and curved, perfect for reaching into flowers.

Habitat Preferences:

- <u>Flower Power</u>: They love gardens, parks, and woodlands with plenty of blooming flowers and feeders. You might see them in unexpected places like beaches or cities during migration!

Ruby-throated Hummingbird

Diet:

- <u>Nectar Ninja & Bug Biter</u>: These little birds mainly sip sweet nectar from flowers and eat tiny insects for protein. You can help them by putting out a feeder with sugar water (no red dye needed!).

Interesting Behaviors:

- <u>Hover Champs</u>: Ruby-throated Hummingbirds can fly in any direction – even backward! Males impress females with fancy dives and loops. They're very protective of their food and will chase away other hummingbirds.

RECORD YOUR SIGHTINGS!

- Date: _____
- Location:_____
- What was the cardinal doing?: _____ _____
- Are there any exciting notes or observations?:_____ _____ _____

Fun Facts:

- <u>Speedy Wings</u>: Their wings beat up to 53 times per second!
- <u>Long-Distance Traveler</u>: They fly over 1,000 miles to Central America for the winter, sometimes nonstop across the Gulf of Mexico!
- <u>Big Eaters</u>: They can eat twice their weight in nectar and insects daily!
- <u>Tiny Toes</u>: Their feet are so small they can't walk, but they can perch and shuffle sideways on branches.

Backyard Tips:
- <u>Feeder Frenzy & Flower Power</u>: To keep them happy, hang feeders with sugar water and plant lots of colorful flowers, such as trumpet creeper and bee balm.
- <u>Nest Nook</u>: Leave some small trees and shrubs in your yard for them to build their tiny, cup-shaped nests.
- <u>Skip the Sprays</u>: Avoid pesticides in your yard so there are plenty of insects for them to eat.

(2) Cedar Waxwing (Bombycilla cedrorum)

Size and Appearance:

- <u>Silky & Crested</u>: Cedar Waxwings are medium-sized with soft, brownish-gray feathers and a relaxed, spiky crest on their heads. They have a black mask and a bright yellow tail tip. But the coolest part - Red, waxy, droplet-like decorations on their wings!

Habitat Preferences:

- <u>Berry Bonanza</u>: Cedar Waxwings love open woods, parks, and gardens, especially near water and places with many fruit trees and bushes.

Diet:

- <u>Fruit Fanatic & Feathered Foodie</u>: These birds mostly eat berries and other fruits but also significantly enjoy insects when raising chicks. They even uniquely share berries!

Interesting Behaviors:

- <u>Friendly Flockers</u>: Cedar Waxwings are super social and hang out in groups year-round. They fly like acrobats and can catch insects mid-air! Listen for their high-pitched trilling calls.

Cedar Waxwing
Image by Jack Bulmer from Pixabay

RECORD YOUR SIGHTINGS!

- Date: _____
- Location: _____
- What was the cardinal doing?: _____ _____
- Are there any exciting notes or observations?: _____ _____ _____

Fun Facts:

- <u>Waxy Wings & Berry Buzz</u>: They get their name from the red waxy things on their wings and their love for cedar berries. Sometimes, they eat fermented berries and get a little tipsy!
- <u>Look-Alike Lovebirds</u>: Male and female Cedar Waxwings look almost identical, unlike many other songbirds.
- <u>Berry Sharing Bonanza</u>: They have a unique way of eating – they pass berries down the line from bird to bird until someone finally eats it!
- <u>Fruity Feasters</u>: Their unique bodies can quickly handle eating a ton of fruit!

Backyard Tips:

- <u>Berry Buffet & Birdbath Bonanza</u>: Plant native berry bushes like serviceberry and dogwood to attract birds. They also like hawthorn, mulberry, and crabapple trees. Set up a birdbath for them to cool off and drink from.
- <u>Nesting Nook</u>: Leave some dense shrubs or small trees in your yard for them to build their cup-shaped nests.
- <u>Shelter Supreme</u>: Plant various trees and bushes to give them places to hide and perch. Mix evergreen and leafy trees for a good home.
- <u>Skip the Sprays</u>: Avoid pesticides so there are plenty of insects for them to eat and their food isn't poisoned.

(3) Snowy Owl (Bubo scandiacus)

Size and Appearance:

- <u>Majestic & Mostly White:</u> Snowy Owls are huge, with white feathers and some black speckles (females have more). Their yellow eyes and round heads with no ear tufts make them stand out.

Habitat Preferences:

- <u>Arctic Adventurers:</u> Snowy Owls live in the freezing Arctic tundra all year round, but in winter, they might fly south to open fields and coasts across Canada and the northern U.S.

Diet:

- <u>Lemming Lovers:</u> These owls mainly hunt small furry animals called lemmings, especially in the Arctic. They also eat other small creatures like rabbits, birds, and seabirds! They hunt all day and night with super eyesight and hearing.

Interesting Behaviors:

- <u>Daytime Hunters:</u> Unlike most owls, Snowy Owls hunt during the day, patiently perching for hours to spot prey. They fly strong and straight with deep wingbeats. Males even do fancy flying shows to impress females!

Snowy Owl

RECORD YOUR SIGHTINGS!
- Date: _____
- Location:_____
- What was the cardinal doing?: _____ _____
- Are there any exciting notes or observations?:_____ _____ _____

Fun Facts:

- Giant of the North: Snowy Owls are some of the most giant owls in North America!
- Feathery Furnace: Their thick feathers keep them warm in the freezing Arctic.
- Travelers on the Hunt: They can fly far to find food, sometimes showing up in unexpected places.
- Quebec's Feathered Star: The Snowy Owl is the official bird of Quebec, Canada!
- Lemming Lunchbox: They can eat up to five lemmings a day, over 1,600 in a year!

Backyard Tips:

- Snowy Spotter: Since they don't usually visit backyards, look for them in areas with open fields (far away, with binoculars!).
- Help Their Food: While you can't attract Snowy Owls directly, making your yard friendly for small mammals like voles and mice can help them indirectly.
- Natural Habitat Hero: Keeping open spaces with few trees in your yard helps small animals live there, which might attract Snowy Owls to the area in the wild.

(4) American Tree Sparrow (Spizelloides arborea)

Size and Appearance:

- Rusty Red & Ground Friend: American Tree Sparrows are small with a rusty brown cap, a black spot on their chest, and a streaky brown back. Look for their long tail and two white wing bars.

Habitat Preferences:

- Brushy Winter Buds love open areas with bushes, often near water. You might see them in fields, backyards, and along roads in winter.

Diet:

- Seedy & Buggy Buffet: These birds eat seeds and insects. In winter, they find seeds on the ground; in summer, they eat bugs and berries.

Interesting Behaviors:

- Sweet Songsters: Listen to their lovely songs, especially in winter! They hang out in groups and hop on the ground to search for food. In summer, they build cozy cup-shaped nests on the ground or in low bushes.

American Tree Sparrow

Image by Hans Toom from Pixabay

RECORD YOUR SIGHTINGS!

- Date: _____
- Location: _____
- What was the cardinal doing?: _____ _____
- Are there any exciting notes or observations?: _____ _____ _____

Fun Facts:

- Grounders, Not Treetoppers: Despite their name, they spend most of their time on the ground!
- Flicking for Food: They have a funny habit of flicking their tails while eating.
- Long-Distance Travelers: These sparrows fly far between their summer homes in the Arctic and their winter spots in the U.S.
- Winter Warmers: Their thick feathers help them survive in super cold weather.
- Cheerful Chirp: Their songs brighten up the winter scenery.

Backyard Tips:

- Ground Grub Grub: Put a feeder with mixed seeds, especially millet, on the ground or a low platform.
- Watery Oasis: Offer a shallow birdbath, especially in winter, to help them stay hydrated.
- Brushy Hideaway: Plant shrubs and leave some brush piles for them to hide in.
- Winter Welcome: While they don't nest in backyards, making your yard welcoming can be a great rest stop for them in the winter.

(5) Yellow-rumped Warbler (Setophaga coronata)

Size and Appearance:

<u>Tiny & Active</u>: Yellow-rumped Warblers are small, busy birds with gray bodies, white chests, and bright yellow patches on their head, rump, and sides. Look for their white wing streaks, too!

Habitat Preferences:

- <u>Forest Friends & City Surprises</u>: In summer, they live in pine forests, but in winter, you might see them in open woods, parks, or even your backyard!

Diet:

- <u>Bug Bouncer & Berry Bonanza</u>: These warblers eat primarily insects in summer, but in winter, they switch to fruits and berries. They can even eat waxy berries like nobody's business!

Interesting Behaviors:

- <u>Flying Feast Finders</u>: Yellow-rumped Warblers are super acrobatic! They flit through branches, catch bugs in mid-air, and even hover to snatch food from leaves. In winter, they join groups of other bird species to find food.

Yellow-rumped Warbler

Photo by <u>Joshua J. Cotten</u> on <u>Unsplash</u>

RECORD YOUR SIGHTINGS!

- Date: _____
- Location: _____
- What was the cardinal doing?: _____ _____
- Are there any exciting notes or observations?: _____ _____ _____

Fun Facts:

- Nicknamed for their namesake! They're called "Butterbutts" because of their bright yellow rump.
- <u>Waxy Winter Wonder</u>: Their unique bodies can digest the wax on berries, so they can stay warm in cold places where other warblers can't go.
- <u>Sweet Songsters</u>: Listen to their lovely trilling song in the summer.
- <u>Double Trouble</u>: Two kinds of Yellow-rumped Warblers – the Myrtle Warbler and Audubon's Warbler – look slightly different.
- <u>Long-Distance Travelers</u>: They fly far south for the winter, from Alaska to Central America!

Backyard Tips:

- <u>Yummy Treats & Watery Oasis</u>: Put out suet, sunflower seeds, and mealworms. Plant berry bushes like bayberry and juniper for a winter feast. Offer a birdbath with fresh water for them to drink and splash in.
- <u>Plant a Feathery Forest</u>: Plant various trees and shrubs to give them places to hide and explore.
- <u>Welcome Winter Warblers</u>: Even if they don't nest in your yard, making it inviting with food and water can be a great rest stop for them in the winter.

Group 9: Social Birds

(1) European Starling (Sturnus vulgari)

Size and Appearance:

- <u>Shiny & Spotted</u>: Starlings are medium-sized with black feathers that shimmer purple and green. In winter, they get white speckles. Their long yellow beak is perfect for grabbing food.

Habitat Preferences:

- <u>City Chums & Field Friends</u>: These super adaptable birds live in cities, farms, forests, and grasslands. You'll often see them in big groups, especially in fields and near people.

European Starling

Image by Aidan Semmens from Pixabay

Diet:

- <u>Bug Bouncer & Leftover Lover</u>: Starlings eat everything from insects and fruits to seeds and food scraps, and their beaks are great at finding hidden treats.

Interesting Behaviors:

- <u>Talkative Tricksters</u>: Starlings can mimic sounds like other birds, animals, and car alarms! They fly in impressive swirling flocks called murmurations, like a living, breathing dance in the sky.

RECORD YOUR SIGHTINGS!

- Date: _____
- Location: _____
- What was the cardinal doing?: _____ _____
- Are there any exciting notes or observations?: _____ _____ _____

Fun Facts:

- <u>Accidental Tourists</u>: Starlings were brought to North America in the 1890s to copy all the birds in Shakespeare's plays!
- <u>Copycat Champions</u> can imitate many sounds, including other birds and human speech!
- <u>Flocking Fury</u>: Thousands of starlings can fly together in perfect harmony, creating beautiful patterns in the sky.
- <u>Nesters in Niches</u>: Starlings build nests in holes – in trees, boxes, or buildings.
- <u>Strong Beaks for Burrowing</u>: Their unique beaks help them dig in the ground to find yummy bugs.

Backyard Tips:

- <u>Feathered Foodies</u>: Provide a variety of food, such as suet, mealworms, peanuts, and sunflower seeds. They also like fruits and leftover bits.
- <u>Watery Oasis</u>: Offer a birdbath with fresh water to keep them hydrated.
- <u>Nest Nook (with Caution)</u>: Leaving a nest box might attract them. But be careful; starlings can be aggressive and compete with other birds for nesting spots.

(2) House Sparrow (Passer domesticus)

Size and Appearance:

- <u>Small & Stocky:</u> House Sparrows are little brown birds with short tails. Males have a black bib, white cheeks, and a brown hat. Females are streaky brown with no bib.

Habitat Preferences:

- <u>City Chums:</u> These birds love living near people in cities, towns, farms, and even your backyard!

Diet:

- <u>Seed Savvy & Scraps Snatcher:</u> House Sparrows eat all sorts of things – seeds, grains, insects, and even leftover bits we drop!

Interesting Behaviors:

- <u>Chatty & Feisty:</u> These social birds chirp and sing a lot but can also be aggressive when protecting their nest or food.

Fun Facts:

- Sparrows of the World: House Sparrows are one of the most common birds on Earth!
- Accidental Tourists: They were brought to North America in the 1800s and are now everywhere!
- Nesters in Niches: House Sparrows build nests in many places, from holes in buildings to birdhouses you put out.
- Dust Devils: They love taking dust baths to keep their feathers clean!
- City Birds: Unlike many birds, House Sparrows don't mind the busy city life.

Backyard Tips:

- Feeder Frenzy: Put out a feeder with seeds like millet, cracked corn, and sunflower seeds. They also like leftover bits and bread crumbs.
- Watery Oasis: Offer a birdbath with fresh water to keep them hydrated.
- Nest Nook (with Caution): Leave a nest box for them, but be aware that house Sparrows can be aggressive and might compete with other birds for nesting spots.

House Sparrow

RECORD YOUR SIGHTINGS!

- Date: _____
- Location: _____
- What was the cardinal doing?: _____ _____
- Are there any exciting notes or observations?: _____ _____ _____

(3) Common Grackle (Quiscalus quiscula)

Common Grackle
Photo by Tina Nord: https://www.pexels.com/photo/close-up-shot-of-a-common-grackle-7532233/

Size and Appearance:

- Long & Iridescent: Common Grackles are medium-sized blackbirds with a long tail. Males are glossy black with a purple head and bronze body, while females are duller.

Habitat Preferences:

- Watery Wanderers: These birds live in many places – open woods, fields, marshes, and even cities and suburbs. They like being near water.

Diet:

- Feedy Frenzy: Grackles eat all sorts of things – seeds, fruits, insects, and even small animals! They are especially fond of feasting in farm fields.

Interesting Behaviors:

- Noisy Neighbors: Grackles are social but can be loud and aggressive, especially when protecting their food or nest. They like to hang out in big groups and make much noise!

RECORD YOUR SIGHTINGS!

- Date: _____
- Location:_____
- What was the cardinal doing?: _____ _____
- Are there any exciting notes or observations?:_____ _____ _____

Fun Facts:

- Rainbow Feathers: Their black feathers shimmer with all the rainbow colors in the sunlight!
- Strong Bill Beak: Their strong beak can crack even tough nuts and acorns open.
- Talkative Tricksters: Sometimes, they can copy sounds like other birds and even human noises!
- Mixed Flockers: They often hang out with other blackbirds, starlings, and cowbirds.
- Ant Party: Grackles like letting ants crawl on them, which might help keep them from pests!

Backyard Tips:

- Food Fiesta (with Caution): Put out seeds, grains, and fruits for them. They love corn and sunflower seeds, but be careful – they might scare away smaller birds.
- Watery Oasis: Offer a birdbath or shallow pond for them to drink and splash around in.
- Treetop Tenants: Plant trees and shrubs for them to roost and nest in. They prefer tall trees for their homes.
- Nesting Nook: You can leave straws and twigs for them to build their nests, but be aware – Grackles can be aggressive towards other birds.

(4) American Crow (Corvus brachyrhynchos)

Size and Appearance:

- **Big & Bold:** American Crows are large black birds with a shiny coat and a fan-shaped tail.

Habitat Preferences:

- **Treetop Townies & City Slickers:** These adaptable birds live in forests, fields, farms, and cities, perching on trees, wires, and rooftops.

Diet:

- **Anything Goes Grub:** Crows are not picky eaters! They enjoy insects, small animals, fruits, nuts, and even leftovers. Their varied diet helps them thrive anywhere.

Interesting Behaviors:

- **Smarter Than Your Average Bird:** Crows are super smart! They can use tools, remember faces, and even mimic sounds like other birds and humans! They love to play, too, like sliding down snowy hills.

American Crow

Image by Jack Bulmer from Pixabay

RECORD YOUR SIGHTINGS!

- Date: _____
- Location: _____
- What was the cardinal doing?: _____ _____
- Are there any exciting notes or observations?: _____ _____ _____

Fun Facts:

- **Brainiac of the Beak:** Crows are some of the most brilliant birds – they can solve puzzles and use tools!
- **Talkative Crows:** They have many different calls, like caws and clicks, to chat with each other.
- **Crow Funerals:** Groups of crows gather around a dead crow, maybe to show respect.
- **Super Recognizers:** Their memory is terrific – they can remember people's faces!
- **Family Flockers:** Crows are social and hang out in big groups, especially in winter.

Backyard Tips:

- **Feeder Frenzy:** Put out peanuts, sunflower seeds, suet, or leftover bits for them on a platform feeder or scattered on the ground. Crows aren't picky!
- **Watery Oasis:** Offer a birdbath or shallow dish for them to drink and splash around in.
- **Treetop Tenants:** Plant trees and shrubs for them to perch and roost in. They prefer tall trees for their homes.
- **Nesting Nook:** Leave straw and twigs for their nests, but be aware – crows can be intelligent and might outsmart other birds for nesting spots.

(5) Red-winged Blackbird (Agelaius phoeniceus)

Size and Appearance:

- Males in Red & Black: Red-winged Blackbirds are medium-sized. Males wear shiny black feathers with bright red and yellow shoulder patches. Females are brown and streaky, looking like big sparrows.

Habitat Preferences:

- Wetland Wonders: These birds love hanging out in marshes, ponds, and lake edges. They also like meadows, fields, and pastures. During the breeding season, they find places with many plants to build their nests.

Diet:

- Anything Goes Grub: Crows are not picky eaters! They enjoy insects, small animals, fruits, nuts, and even leftovers. Their varied diet helps them thrive anywhere.

Interesting Behaviors:

- Bossy Birds: Red-winged Blackbirds can be aggressive, especially the males. They chase away other birds, even big ones, to protect their territory. They also have a loud, distinct call to warn others to stay away.

Fun Facts:

- Singing for Love & Space: Male Red-winged Blackbirds sing songs to show off their territory and attract mates.
- Secret Nest Builders: The females build hidden nests in thick plants near water.
- Winter Flockers: In winter, they group in large flocks, sometimes with other blackbirds, starlings, and grackles.

Backyard Tips:

- Food Fiesta: Put sunflower, cracked corn, and millet seeds on a platform feeder or scatter them on the ground to attract them.
- Watery Oasis: Offer a birdbath or shallow dish with fresh water for them to drink and bathe in. Keep it clean!

Red-winged Blackbird

Image by Howard Walsh from Pixabay

RECORD YOUR SIGHTINGS!

- Date: _____
- Location: _____
- What was the cardinal doing?: _____ _____
- Are there any exciting notes or observations?: _____ _____ _____

Group 10: Birds with Unique Features

(1) Belted Kingfisher (Megaceryle Alcyon)

Size and Appearance:

- <u>Big Head, Big Bill:</u> Belted Kingfishers are medium-sized with a blocky head, a shaggy crest, and a long, sharp bill. Males are blue-gray with a white bib and a blue chest band. Females have an extra rusty belly band.

Habitat Preferences:

- <u>Water Watchers:</u> These birds live near clean water – rivers, streams, lakes, and coasts. They like places with cliffs or banks to make their nests.

Diet:

- <u>Fishy Feasts:</u> Belted Kingfishers mainly eat fish, diving headfirst to catch them! They also eat frogs, crayfish, insects, and even small animals. Their sharp eyes help them spot prey from afar.

Interesting Behaviors:

- <u>Rattling Reclaimers:</u> They use a loud rattle to defend their territory. They perch on branches or wires above the water, waiting for lunch to swim by. They dig long tunnels in banks for their nests.

Belted Kingfisher

RECORD YOUR SIGHTINGS!

- Date: _____
- Location:_____
- What was the cardinal doing?: _____ _____
- Are there any exciting notes or observations?:_____ _____ _____

Fun Facts:
- <u>Hover Hunters:</u> Belted Kingfishers hover in the air before diving to catch fish – like a helicopter with a beak!
- <u>Eyelid Armor</u>: They have noteworthy eyelids that protect their eyes when they go underwater.
- <u>Team Tunnelers:</u> Both mom and dad Kingfisher help dig their nest tunnel.
- <u>Helpless Hatchlings:</u> Baby Kingfishers are born blind and need their parents' care until they can fly.

Backyard Tips:

- <u>Fishy Attraction (Maybe):</u> While they love fish, these Kingfishers likely won't visit feeders. They might check out if you have a clean pond with small fish!
- <u>Watery Oasis:</u> A pond or stream with fish can attract them, but make sure the water is clean.
- <u>Natural Nest Banks:</u> If you have natural banks or cliffs on your property, leave them alone! Kingfishers might nest there. You can be quiet near these areas during the breeding season.
- <u>Nesting Neighbors</u> : If you live near a body of water with banks, you might be lucky enough to have Belted Kingfishers nesting nearby. Keep it peaceful for them!

(2) Red-headed Woodpecker(Melanerpes erythrocephalus)

Size and Appearance:

- Red-headed & Black-winged: Red-headed woodpeckers are medium-sized with bright red heads, white bellies, and black backs with white wing patches.

Habitat Preferences:

- Open Woodland Whizzes: These woodpeckers live in open woods, forest edges, orchards, and farms. They love dead trees and stumps for nesting and finding food.

Red-headed Woodpecker
Photo by A. G. Rosales:
https://www.pexels.com/photo/red-headed-woodpecker-with-food-17575248/

Diet:

- Insect Catchers & Stashers: Red-headed Woodpeckers eat insects, fruits, nuts, and even small animals. They're super acrobatic and can catch insects in mid-air! They're also unique because they hide food like acorns for later.

Interesting Behaviors:

- Flying Food Finders: These woodpeckers can fly like little acrobats and snatch insects right out of the air!

RECORD YOUR SIGHTINGS!

- Date: _____
- Location:_____
- What was the cardinal doing?: _____ _____
- Are there any exciting notes or observations?:_____ _____ _____

Fun Facts:

- Redhead Party of Two: Both male and female Red-headed Woodpeckers have the same bright red head!
- Recycled Homes: They often use the same nest hole year after year.
- Forest Helpers: These woodpeckers help keep the forest healthy by eating bugs and spreading seeds.

Backyard Tips:

- Feeder Frenzy: Put out suet, peanuts, sunflower seeds, and fruits to attract them. They also like feeders with cracked corn and nuts.
- Watery Oasis: Offer a birdbath with fresh water, especially during hot weather.
- Snag Sanctuary: Leave dead trees in your yard if possible. They use them for nesting and finding food. You can also put up woodpecker nest boxes.
- Nesting Nook: They prefer holes in dead trees for nesting. If you have suitable trees, avoid cutting them down. Keep it quiet near their nests so they feel safe.

(3) Eastern Phoebe (Sayornis phoebe)

Size and Appearance:

- Small & Plain: Eastern Phoebes are small, brown-gray birds with a white belly. They don't have many fancy markings but often puff their head feathers like a mini-mohawk.

Habitat Preferences:

- Open Space Explorers: These birds live in woods, farms, suburbs, and near water. They like places with open areas to catch food and sheltered spots to build nests, sometimes under bridges or houses!

Diet:

- Insect Eater with a Berry Bonus: Eastern Phoebes mainly eat insects like flies and beetles. They might also eat some fruits, especially in winter when insects are harder to find.

Interesting Behaviors:

- Wagging While Waiting: These birds wag their tails up and down, especially when they are perched and looking for food.
- "Phoebe" Calls the Place: They have a distinct call that sounds like their name – Phoebe! They use this call to chat with each other and keep other birds away from their territory.

Fun Facts:

- First-Ever Banded Bird: Eastern Phoebes were the first birds ever to be tagged with a little band in North America, way back in 1804!
- Early Spring Travelers: These birds are some of the first to return north in the spring, before many other songbirds.
- Catchers in Mid-Air: Eastern Phoebes are excellent at catching flying insects. They dart out from a perch and snatch their prey in a flash!

Backyard Tips:

- Insect Buffet (Not Really): While they mainly catch insects, you can offer them mealworms as a treat. Planting bushes with berries can also give them a winter snack.
- Watery Oasis: Put out a birdbath or small pond for them to drink and splash around in.

Eastern Phoebe

Image by Megan Zopf from Pixabay

RECORD YOUR SIGHTINGS!

- Date: _____
- Location:_____
- What was the cardinal doing?: _____ _____
- Are there any exciting notes or observations?:_____ _____ _____

(4) White-breasted Nuthatch (Sitta carolinensis)

Size and Appearance:

- Black Cap & White Chest: White-breasted Nuthatches are small with a black cap, white face and chest, and blue-gray back. Their short tail and long, curved bills help them climb and eat.

Habitat Preferences:

- Forest Feasters: These birds live in mature forests, especially with oak trees. They also visit feeders and yards with big trees.

Diet:

- Insect Inspectors & Nut Nashers: White-breasted Nuthatches eat insects, spiders, seeds, and nuts. They climb down trees looking for food and even store nuts for winter! They wedge nuts in cracks and smash them open with their strong beaks.

Interesting Behaviors:

- Headfirst Flyers: These amazing birds climb down trees upside down! They search nooks and crannies for insects and look for places to stash their nuts.
- Yanky Talkers: Listen for their loud "yank-yank" calls – that's how you know they're around!

Fun Facts:

- They can hang upside down like a tiny gymnast!
- They're like tiny carpenters, hammering nuts open in bark.
- They find a mate and stick together all year long.
- Their name, "Nuthatch," tells you what they love to eat – nuts!

Backyard Tips:

- Feeder Frenzy: To attract them, put out sunflower seeds, peanuts, suet, and mealworms. They love big seeds and nuts for storage.
- Watery Oasis: Offer a birdbath with fresh water, especially in winter.
- Treetop Town: Plant trees and leave dead branches in your yard for them to climb and nest in. They also like bushy areas to hide.

White-breasted Nuthatch

Image by Jack Bulmer from Pixabay

RECORD YOUR SIGHTINGS!

- Date: _____
- Location: _____
- What was the cardinal doing?: _____
- Are there any exciting notes or observations?: _____

Image by Veronika Andrews from Pixabay

(5) Carolina Wren (Thryothorus ludovicianus)

Size and Appearance:

- Reddish-brown & Round: Carolina Wrens are small and plump with a reddish-brown back, orange belly, and a white stripe above their eye. Their short, rounded wings and curved bills help them hop around.

Habitat Preferences:

- Forest & Garden Friends: These wrens live in forests, swamps, and your backyard! They love bushy areas to hide and build nests.

Diet:

- Insect Inspectors & Berry Nibblers: Carolina Wrens mainly eat insects and spiders but enjoy fruits and seeds, especially in winter.

Interesting Behaviors:

- Singing the Kettle Song: Listen for their loud, straightforward song that sounds like a teapot – "teakettle-teakettle-teakettle"!
- Curious & Hopping: These wrens are active and love exploring for food. They hop around in the bushes and might even check you out!

Carolina Wren
Image by Jack Bulmer from Pixabay

RECORD YOUR SIGHTINGS!

- Date: _____
- Location: _____
- What was the cardinal doing?: _____ _____
- Are there any exciting notes or observations?: _____ _____ _____

Fun Facts:

- Year-Round Residents: Carolina Wrens don't migrate – they stay in the same spot all year.
- Family Teamwork: Mom and Dad Wren work together to build their nest and raise their young.
- Singing Stars: They have an extensive song repertoire with up to 40 tunes!
- Lifelong Lovebirds: Carolina Wrens often mate for life and stay together.
- Bold Neighbors: These wrens aren't shy and might even nest near your house!

Backyard Tips:

- Yummy Treats: To attract them, put out suet, peanut butter, mealworms, and sunflower seeds. They also like fruits like raisins and berries.
- Watery Oasis: Offer a birdbath with fresh water, especially during hot weather.
- Bushy Hideaways: Plant shrubs and vines to give them places to hide and build nests. They also like brush piles.

Fun Corner 4

Quiz Corner

1. Which bird is known for its bright red plumage in males and brownish-red plumage in females?
A) Blue Jay   B) Northern Cardinal   C) Baltimore Oriole   D) American Robin

2. What color are male American Goldfinches during the summer?
A) Olive-brown   B) Bright yellow   C) Blue with white markings   D) Bright orange and black

3. Which small bird has a black cap and bib with white cheeks?
A) House Finch   B) Dark-eyed Junco   C) Black-capped Chickadee   D) Song Sparrow

4. Which woodpecker is characterized by a black-and-white coloration and small size?
A) Downy Woodpecker   B) Hairy Woodpecker   C) Red-bellied Woodpecker   D) Pileated Woodpecker

5. What distinctive feature does the Great Blue Heron have?
A) Greenhead   B) Large, gray-blue body with a long neck   C) Black head and neck with white cheeks   D) Black body with a white bill

6. Which bird of prey is known for its small size and colorful plumage?
A) Red-tailed Hawk   B) Great Horned Owl   C) American Kestrel   D) Bald Eagle

7. Which ground feeder has a pale brown body with a long, pointed tail?
A) Northern Bobwhite   B) Eastern Towhee   C) Wild Turkey   D) Mourning Dove

8. Which singing bird has gray feathers with white wing patches?
A) Northern Mockingbird   B) House Wren   C) Gray Catbird   D) Eastern Meadowlark

9. What is a distinctive feature of the Cedar Waxwing?
A) Green with a red throat   B) Brown with a yellow-tipped tail and red wing spots   C) White with black markings   D) Gray with a yellow rump and sides

10. Which social bird is entirely black?
A) European Starling   B) House Sparrow   C) American Crow   D) Red-winged Blackbird

Solution: Quiz Corner

Answers:
1. B) Northern Cardinal
2. B) Bright yellow
3. C) Black-capped Chickadee
4. A) Downy Woodpecker
5. B) Large, gray-blue body with a long neck
6. C) American Kestrel
7. D) Mourning Dove
8. A) Northern Mockingbird
9. B) Brown with a yellow-tipped tail and red wing spots
10. C) American Crow

Why do birds fly south in the winter?

Because it's too far to walk!

Why did the little bird get in trouble at school?

For tweeting on a test!

Chapter 5: The Amazing World of Birds

Welcome to the amazing world of birds! Birds are some of the most fascinating creatures on Earth. In this chapter, we'll explore their superpowers, how they help the environment, and the challenges they face. Get ready for an exciting journey into the lives of our feathered friends!

Superpowers of Birds

Flight

- Birds rule the sky! Their lightweight skeletons, strong muscles, and uniquely crafted feathers make them exceptional aviators. Were you aware that the Peregrine Falcon can plunge at speeds exceeding 240 miles per hour, faster than a racing car?

Fun Fact:

- Hummingbirds can hover in mid-air and even fly backward; they beat their wings approximately 50 times per second!

Migration

- Many birds migrate, traveling thousands of miles between their breeding and wintering grounds. For example, the Arctic Tern flies from the Arctic to Antarctica annually—about 25,000 miles!

Anecdote:

- One famous migratory bird is the Bar-tailed Godwit. It holds the record for the longest non-stop flight, traveling over 7,000 miles from Alaska to New Zealand without taking a break!

Image by 승목 오 from Pixabay

Camouflage

Birds use camouflage to blend into their surroundings and avoid predators. The Eastern screech owl, for example, has feathers that look just like tree bark, making it nearly invisible when it perches on a branch.

Trivia:

- The Common Potoo is a master of disguise. It looks like a broken tree branch when it sits still during the day.

A common potoo masquerading as a branch
By Chiswick Chap - Own work, CC BY-SA 3.0,
https://commons.wikimedia.org/w/index.php?curid=30810962

Superpower	Example Bird	Amazing Fact
Flight	Peregrine Falcon	Can dive at speeds over 240 mph
Migration	Arctic Tern	Travels about 25,000 miles each year
Camouflage	Eastern Screech-Owl	Feathers resemble tree bark

Birds and the Environment

Birds play a vital role in our ecosystem. They help control pests, pollinate plants, and spread seeds. Without birds, our world would be a very different place!

Birds and the Environment

Birds play a vital role in our ecosystem. They help control pests, pollinate plants, and spread seeds. Without birds, our world would be a very different place!

Pest Control

- Birds like the American Kestrel eat insects and rodents, keeping their populations in check. This helps farmers protect their crops without using harmful pesticides.

Example:

- The Barn Owl family can eat over 3,000 rodents in one breeding season!

Pollination

Hummingbirds and other nectar-feeding birds help pollinate flowers. When they sip nectar, pollen sticks to their feathers and beaks, and they carry it to the next flower they visit.

Seed Dispersal

Birds such as the Blue Jay help plants grow by spreading seeds. They eat fruits and berries and later expel the seeds in different locations, allowing new plants to sprout.

Trivia:

- The Clark's Nutcracker can bury up to 30,000 seeds annually, helping forests regenerate!

Threats Birds Face

Unfortunately, birds face many threats that endanger their survival. Understanding these challenges is essential for us to help protect them.

Habitat Loss

As humans build more homes, roads, and farms, birds lose the places they need to live, breed, and find food. Forests, wetlands, and grasslands are disappearing, leaving birds with fewer safe-havens.

Example:

- The Ivory-billed Woodpecker is critically endangered due to the loss of its forest habitat.

Pollution

Pollution from chemicals, plastics, and oil spills can harm birds. For example, seabirds often mistake plastic pieces for food, which can be deadly.

Anecdote:

- In 1989, the Exxon Valdez oil spill in Alaska killed hundreds of thousands of seabirds.

Climate Change

Climate change affects birds by altering their habitats and food sources. If temperatures change too quickly, some birds may not be able to migrate to their traditional breeding or feeding grounds.

Trivia:

- Although not a bird, the American pika is an example of a species severely affected by climate change, serving as a reminder of the broader impacts on wildlife.

Quiz Corner

1. What adaptation helps birds fly?
   A) Hollow bones   B) Heavy bones   C) Webbed feet   D) Strong jaws

2. Which bird is famous for its long migration from the Arctic to the Antarctic?
   A) Penguin   B) Arctic Tern   C) Bald Eagle   D) Hummingbird

3. What is camouflage used for by birds?
   A) Attracting mates   B) Finding food   C) Hiding from predators   D) Singing louder

4. Which bird has the superpower of seeing ultraviolet light?
   A) Sparrow   B) Eagle   C) Owl   D) Hummingbird

5. What is the primary purpose of bird migration?
   A) To find new friends   B) To escape from predators   C) To find better food and breeding grounds
   D) To visit different countries

6. How do birds help in controlling insect populations?
   A) By eating them   B) By scaring them away   C) By building nests   D) By singing

7. What role do birds play in pollination?
   A) They eat the flowers.   B) They spread pollen while feeding on nectar   C) They water the plants
   D) They protect the flowers

8. Which bird is known for spreading seeds through its droppings, helping plant growth?
   A) Crow   B) Eagle   C) Pigeon   D) Owl

9. What is one of the biggest threats to bird habitats?
   A) Planting more trees   B) Habitat loss due to deforestation   C) Creating bird sanctuaries
   D) Birdwatching

10. How does climate change affect birds?
    A) It makes them fly faster.   B) It changes their migration patterns and food availability
    C) It makes them sing more   D) It gives them more feathers

Solution: Quiz Corner

Answers:
1. A) Hollow bones
2. B) Arctic Tern
3. C) Hiding from predators
4. D) Hummingbird
5. C) To find better food and breeding grounds
6. A) By eating them
7. B) They spread pollen while feeding on nectar
8. C) Pigeon
9. B) Habitat loss due to deforestation
10. B) It changes their migration patterns and food availability

What kind of music do crows like?

Caw-ntry music!

Why did the bicycle fall over?

Because it was two tired!

Keeping a Birding Journal

Keeping a birding journal is like becoming a detective of the bird world! You get to record your observations, sketch the birds you see, and log your sightings. Here's how you can start:

What to Record

- Date and Time: Note when you spotted the bird. This helps track bird activity throughout the year.
- Location: Write down where you saw the bird. Different birds prefer different habitats.
- Weather Conditions: Was it sunny, cloudy, rainy, or snowy? Weather can affect bird behavior.
- Bird Description: Note the bird's size, color, and unique markings.
- Behavior: Was the bird flying, perching, singing, or feeding?

Fun Fact

Did you know that John James Audubon, a famous bird artist, kept detailed journals of his bird observations? His notes and sketches are still used by birdwatchers today!

By John Syme – The White House Historical Association, Public Domain, https://commons.wikimedia.org/w/index.php?curid=9359700

Sample Journal Entry

Date	Time	Location	Weather	Bird Description	Behavior
June 15	9:00 AM	Backyard Garden	Sunny	Small bird, bright red feathers	Singing on a tree
September 10	4:30 PM	Local Park	Cloudy	Medium-sized bird, black and white	Pecking at the ground

Bird Photography Basics

Taking great pictures of birds is an exciting way to document your birding adventures. Here are some tips to get you started:

Essential Tips

- Use a Zoom Lens: Birds can be shy, so a camera with a good zoom lens helps you get close-up shots without disturbing them.
- Stay Quiet and Still: Birds are easily scared, so move slowly and quietly.
- Focus on the Eyes: A sharp focus on the bird's eyes makes your photos look professional.
- Be Patient: Sometimes, you have to wait for the perfect shot. Bring a snack and enjoy the wait!

Fun Fact

Noah Strycker holds the world record for the most bird species photographed in one year, having documented 6,042 bird species in 2015!

Photography Challenge

Try to capture a picture of a bird in flight. It's challenging but can be very rewarding! Look for birds that frequently take off, like sparrows or pigeons.

Attract More Birds to Your Backyard

Creating a bird-friendly backyard is a fun way to enjoy bird-watching without leaving home. Here are some projects and activities you can try:

Build a Pinecone Bird Feeder

<u>Materials:</u>

- Pine cone

- Peanut butter
- Birdseed
- String

Steps:

- Tie a string around the top of the pine cone.
- Spread peanut butter all over the pine cone.
- Roll the pine cone in birdseed until it's well coated.
- Hang the feeder from a tree branch.

Create a Bird Bath

Materials:

- Large shallow dish or saucer
- Stones or pebbles

Steps:

- Place the dish in your garden where it can be easily seen by birds.
- Add stones or pebbles to the dish to give birds a place to perch.
- Fill the dish with water, and keep it clean and filled regularly.

Plant Bird-Friendly Plants

Certain plants can attract more birds to your yard. Here are some bird-friendly plants to consider:

- Sunflowers: Attract finches and sparrows.
- Coneflowers: Loved by goldfinches.
- Holly: Provides berries for many birds in winter.
- Milkweed: Attracts hummingbirds.

Fun Fact

Hummingbirds can flap their wings about 70 times per second! Planting red or tubular flowers can help attract these tiny acrobats to your garden.

Trivia Time!

1. What type of bird can sleep while flying?
   - A) Owl
   - B) Swift
   - C) Pigeon
   - D) Robin

   Answer 1 : B) Swift

2. Which bird is known for mimicking the sounds of other birds and even humans?
   - A) Parrot
   - B) Crow
   - C) Mockingbird
   - D) Sparrow

   Answer 2 : C) Mockingbird

Conclusion

Becoming a birding master takes practice and patience, but it's enriching. By keeping a birding journal, taking great photos, and creating a bird-friendly backyard, you'll learn a lot about birds and help them thrive. Happy bird watching!

What do you call a competition between robins?
A worm war!

What did the bird say when it bumped into a window?
"Tweet, that hurt!"

Quiz Corner

1. What do you think you should include in a birding journal?
A) Favorite colors   B) Observations, sketches, and sightings   C) Recipes for bird food   D) Photos of other animals

2. Why is it helpful to sketch birds in your journal?
A) To practice drawing   B) To remember what the bird looked like   C) To fill up pages   D) To make the journal look pretty

3. What is the primary purpose of logging sightings in a birding journal?
A) To show off to friends   B) To keep track of birds you've seen   C) To win a birdwatching contest   D) To compare with other journals

4. What is a good tip for taking clear pictures of birds?
A) Shout to get their attention   B) Use a fast shutter speed   C) Use a bright flash   D) Stand very close to the bird

5. When is the best time to take pictures of birds?
A) At night   B) In the middle of the day   C) Early morning or late afternoon   D) During a storm

6. What should you focus on when photographing a bird?
A) The background   B) The bird's surroundings   C) The bird's eyes   D) The sky

7. What food can you put out to attract various birds?
A) Candy   B) Bread crumbs   C) Sunflower seeds   D) Cheese

8. Which of these is a fun project to attract birds to your backyard?
A) Building a sandcastle   B) Planting bird-friendly plants   C) Painting rocks   D) Setting up a trampoline

9. Why is providing water meaningful for attracting birds?
A) Birds like to swim   B) Water attracts insects for the birds to eat   C) Birds need water to drink and bathe   D) Water keeps the birds cool

10. What is an excellent place to hang a bird feeder to attract birds?
A) In a dark, hidden corner   B) Near a window   C) High in a tree or near bushes   D) On the ground

Fun Corner 6

Solution: Quiz Corner

Answers:
1. B) Observations, sketches, and sightings
2. B) To remember what the bird looked like
3. B) To keep track of birds you've seen
4. B) Use a fast shutter speed
5. C) Early morning or late afternoon
6. C) The bird's eyes
7. C) Sunflower seeds
8. B) Planting bird-friendly plants
9. C) Birds need water to drink and bathe
10. C) High in a tree or near bushes

Why did the birdwatcher wear sunglasses while looking for owls?

Because he couldn't owl-ways see them at night!

Why did the baby woodpecker have a headache?

Because he kept pecking the wrong tree!

Glossary 1: Birding Terms

- <u>Adaptation</u>: A particular trait or behavior that helps a bird survive in its environment. For example, ducks have webbed feet to help them swim.

- <u>Avian</u>: Relating to birds. For example, avian species means bird species.

- <u>Bird of Prey:</u> Birds that hunt and eat other animals. Examples include eagles, hawks, and owls.

- <u>Camouflage</u>: Colors or patterns that help a bird blend in with its surroundings to avoid predators. For example, a brown bird might blend in with tree bark.

- <u>Clutch</u>: The group of eggs laid by a bird at one time. For example, a robin's clutch might contain 3-5 eggs.

- <u>Crest</u>: A tuft of feathers on a bird's head. For example, the Northern Cardinal has a noticeable crest.

- <u>Down</u>: The soft, fluffy feathers found under the outer feathers of birds, especially in chicks, keep them warm.

- <u>Feeder</u>: A device filled with food for birds, often placed in backyards to attract them.

- <u>Fledgling</u>: A young bird that has just acquired its feathers and is learning to fly.

- <u>Habitat</u>: The natural environment where a bird lives, such as forests, wetlands, or grasslands.

- <u>Insectivore</u>: A bird that primarily eats insects. For example, swallows are insectivores.

- <u>Migrate</u> The seasonal movement of birds from one place to another, usually to find food or to breed. For example, many birds migrate south for the winter.

- <u>Nest</u>: A structure built by birds to lay eggs and raise their young. Nests can be made of twigs, leaves, mud, and other materials.

- <u>Ornithologist</u>: A scientist who studies birds.

- <u>Perch</u>: A place where a bird sits or rests, such as a branch or a bird feeder.

Glossary 1 Continued.....

- <u>Plumage</u>: The feathers covering a bird's body. Plumage can vary by species and sometimes changes with the seasons.

- <u>Preen</u>: The act of a bird grooming its feathers to keep them in good condition. Birds use their beaks to preen.

- <u>Raptor</u>: Another term for birds of prey. Raptors have sharp talons and beaks to catch and eat their prey.

- <u>Roost</u>: A place where birds rest or sleep. Birds may roost in trees, on cliffs, or in man-made structures.

- <u>Songbird</u>: Birds that are known for their singing abilities. Examples include sparrows, robins, and finches.

- <u>Talons</u>: The sharp claws of birds of prey. Talons help them catch and hold onto their prey.

- <u>Territory</u>: An area that a bird defends against others of the same species. Birds may sing or display to keep others out of their territory.

- <u>Wingspan</u>: The distance from the tip of one wing to the tip of the other when a bird spreads its wings.

- <u>Wading Bird</u>: Birds that search for food in shallow water, such as herons and egrets. They usually have long legs and necks.

- <u>Zygodactyl</u>: A type of bird foot where two toes point forward and two toes point backward, common in woodpeckers and parrots.

Glossary 2 : Online Resources & Birding Apps for Kids

Resource/App	Description	Website/App
eBird	A great tool for logging bird sightings and exploring data from birdwatchers around the world.	https://ebird.org
Merlin Bird ID	An app that helps identify birds by photos, sounds, and a few simple questions.	https://merlin.allaboutbirds.org
Audubon Bird Guide	Provides detailed information on over 800 species of birds in North America.	https://www.audubon.org/app
BirdNET	An app that identifies birds by their songs and calls.	https://birdnet.cornell.edu
Project FeederWatch	A citizen science project where kids can count birds at their feeders and contribute to a scientific study.	https://feederwatch.org
National Geographic Kids	Offers fun facts, games, and articles about birds and other animals	https://kids.nationalgeographic.com

YouTube Channel	Description	Link
Nature Cat	Fun and educational videos about nature, including birdwatching, aimed at kids.	https://www.youtube.com/user/NatureCatShow
SciShow Kids	Educational videos about various science topics, including bird behavior and habitats.	https://www.youtube.com/user/scishowkids
The Cornell Lab of Ornithology	Educational videos about birds, birdwatching, and bird conservation.	https://www.youtube.com/user/LabofOrnithology
PBS KIDS	Engaging and informative videos for kids on various nature topics, including birdwatching.	https://www.youtube.com/user/pbskids
Kids Learning Tube	Fun animated videos teaching kids about different bird species and their characteristics.	https://www.youtube.com/user/kidslearningtube
Wild Kratts	Entertaining videos about wildlife adventures, including birds, aimed at kids.	https://www.youtube.com/user/wildkrattsofficial

Conclusion: Your Birdwatching Adventure Awaits!

Congratulations on completing "The Ultimate Bird Watching Book for Kids: Explore, Learn, and Journal 50 Amazing Backyard Birds"! You've embarked on an exciting journey into the world of birds, and we hope you've discovered just how fascinating and fun birdwatching can be.

Part 1: Get Ready to Be a Birder! You started by learning the basics of birdwatching, from understanding what birdwatching is to gear up for your birding adventures. You discovered why birds are so cool and how anyone can become a birder. Birding is a lifelong adventure; there's always something new to learn!

Part 2: Meet Your Feathered Neighbors! In this section, you met 50 common backyard birds. You learned their size, appearance, habitat preferences, diet, and interesting behaviors. You recorded sightings and observations with your birding journal, becoming a true backyard bird detective!

Part 3: Let's Go Birding! You created the perfect backyard bird oasis, making your yard a haven for feathered friends. You explored local parks and nature trails and even learned how to participate in citizen science projects. Birdwatching can happen anywhere, whether in your backyard or on vacation.

Part 4: The Amazing World of Birds This part took you deeper into the world of birds, uncovering their unique superpowers like flight, migration, and camouflage. You also learned about birds' vital role in the ecosystem and the threats they face from habitat loss, pollution, and climate change. Understanding these challenges is the first step in helping to protect our feathered friends.

Part 5: Become a Birding Master! You're now equipped to take your birding skills to the next level. You know how to keep a detailed birding journal, take great bird photos, and attract more birds to your backyard with fun projects and activities. Your passion and knowledge can inspire others to appreciate and protect birds.

Keep Exploring!

Your birdwatching adventure doesn't end here. Keep exploring, observing, and learning about birds. Share your knowledge with friends and family, and inspire them to join you in birdwatching. Remember, every bird you see and every note you take helps scientists learn more about our feathered friends and how to protect them.

Final Thoughts

Birdwatching is not just a hobby; it's a way to connect with nature, learn about the environment, and contribute to conservation efforts. By becoming a birdwatcher, you're playing a vital role in protecting the natural world and ensuring that birds continue to thrive for generations.

Thank you for joining us on this fantastic birdwatching journey. We hope you continue to enjoy the beauty and wonder of birds. Happy birding!

Bonus!

Don't forget to check out the glossary of birding terms and the online resources and birding apps for kids to enhance your birdwatching skills and knowledge further.
Happy Birdwatching!

Please let us know how we're doing by leaving us a review.